T0381158

SECRET
TREASURES
From
PSALMS

*Using Psalms 1–24 as a map to the treasure of God's heart
toward you and as a key to unlock insight and daily application
of concepts that affect your life and community*

RACHEL RYAN

WESTBOW
PRESS®
A DIVISION OF THOMAS NELSON
& ZONDERVAN

WestBow Press books may be ordered through booksellers or by contacting:

WestBow Press
A Division of Thomas Nelson & Zondervan
1663 Liberty Drive
Bloomington, IN 47403
www.westbowpress.com
844-714-3454

Scripture taken from the Amplified Bible, Copyright © 1954, 1958, 1962, 1964, 1965, 1987 by The Lockman Foundation. Used with permission.

Scripture quotations taken from The Holy Bible, New International Version® NIV® Copyright © 1973 1978 1984 2011 by Biblica, Inc. TM. Used by permission. All rights reserved worldwide.

Scripture taken from The Message. Copyright © 1993, 1994, 1995, 1996, 2000, 2001, 2002. Used by permission of NavPress Publishing Group.

ISBN: 978-1-6642-7091-6 (sc)
ISBN: 978-1-6642-7092-3 (e)

Library of Congress Control Number: 2022912074

Print information available on the last page.

WestBow Press rev. date: 9/27/2022

I am the wife of a hardworking and faithful man and mother of two wonderful children. I earned my bachelor's in psychology, and I have been a high school teacher for over 15 years teaching reading, government, economics, and psychology. I was the overseer of Sunday school at my former church, which is a satellite campus from the church I was raised in and attended for over 15 years. I accepted Jesus into my heart when I was a young child in a chapel service at the Christian school I attended. I was baptized shortly after. I remember that I was so short the pastor had to lift me up for the congregation to see me. Though I have made plenty of mistakes in my lifetime, I have never strayed from my faith in God, and He has proven Himself faithful over and over again.

I am not a formally trained biblical scholar, so I had to do much research throughout this endeavor. I prayed throughout each step of the process and believe that the Holy Spirit has led me in writing this brief study of Psalms. My thoughts and the concepts highlighted are not revolutionary, nor are they the only interpretation of the verses discussed. However, I feel that they are extremely important and applicable to our daily lives and what we see going on in the world around us today.

I am so happy you have decided to join me on this journey through Psalms 1-24. There are so many jewels to be unearthed as we travel through joy and heartache, distress and victory with David. What he learns through his experience is what we are supposed to learn as well. He teaches us who God really is and how we are supposed to respond to Him. He shows us how to live and how not to live and the consequences of our choices. He teaches us how to have a closer, more genuine relationship with God, and how to rely on God as our source.

This study can be used in several ways: as a personal Bible study or daily devotion, as a foundation for Sunday school lessons and discussion, or as a weekly or monthly small group Bible study. One of the unique features of this study includes having the full text of scriptures being discussed right there on the page to make referencing and rereading it faster and easier. I rely on the Amplified version because of the built-in word studies and explanations. I love the depth these features bring to the Word, which is alive and multi-faceted like a diamond.

I encourage you to read through the Psalm being discussed first, and then re-read the verses as they are discussed. There is also an opportunity to read them again throughout the week in the daily topic based mini study. You will have read each of these Psalms three times by the end of your study if you follow this format. Some other features are the side notes, which give some interesting facts and websites to visit, and at the end of each chapter is a prayer based on verses from the Psalm being studied. Finally, there are additional verses and questions after the initial study of the chapter to explore concepts from that chapter and allow for your personal response or group discussion.

May God bless you and speak to you no matter how you choose to use this book. May you grow in your love and trust of God and be strengthened by His Word.

Week 1 Day 1: Psalm 1

¹ Blessed (happy, fortunate, prosperous, and enviable) is the man who walks and lives not in the counsel of the ungodly [following their advice, their plans and purposes], nor stands [submissive and inactive] in the path where sinners walk, nor sits down [to relax and rest] where the scornful [and the mockers] gather.
² But his delight and desire are in the law of the Lord, and on His law (the precepts, the instructions, the teachings of God) he habitually meditates (ponders and studies) by day and by night.
³ And he shall be like a tree firmly planted [and tended] by the streams of water, ready to bring forth its fruit in its season; its leaf also shall not fade or wither; and everything he does shall prosper [and come to maturity].
⁴ Not so the wicked [those disobedient and living without God are not so]. But they are like the chaff [worthless, dead, without substance] which the wind drives away.
⁵ Therefore the wicked [those disobedient and living without God] shall not stand [justified] in the judgment, nor [b]sinners in the congregation of the righteous [those who are upright and in right standing with God].

Blessed- let's start there. The entire book of Psalms starts with the word "blessed." Psalms takes the reader through almost every emotion a person can experience— joy, confidence, fear, depression, guilt and so much more, but the overarching theme is a deep faith in God's love for us no matter where we are or what we have done. The book of Psalms reflects the message of the entire Bible, and this message is woven in the Psalms through poetry, songs, meditations, and prayers. As we study the Word of God and learn more about this great love, we find that we are truly blessed.

To be blessed is to be happy, prosperous, and fortunate. To live a blessed life is enviable, meaning that it is to be desired, and it is desirable to others when they look at our blessed life. There are many preachers teaching prosperity. Don't shy away from that, just make sure you follow the scriptures and study them in context. Psalm 1:2 tells us to meditate and study God's Word as a regular habit. You should know the Word well enough to know if the teaching you are listening to is biblical. Financial blessings are absolutely a part of the Christian life, but prosperity can come in many forms. I want to encourage you to seek more than just financial blessings as you walk through this life. I regularly pray for spiritual, physical, and financial blessings. I desire all three, and this is biblical. How do we obtain blessings so great that our lives are prosperous and enviable? Keep reading verse 1 to find out.

The Psalmist begins with a list of don'ts, which tends to be what religion is known for and what deters some people following the Christian faith. I want to advise you not to focus on the don'ts of the Bible. They are there to protect you and are important, but God wants us to focus on the do's. Following the do list will automatically steer you away from the do not list. Keep reading Psalm 1 to see what I mean.

A person who lives a blessed life does not follow the same path as the ungodly (vs. 1). He or she does not follow the ungodly person's advice, nor do they stand submissively or inactively with sinners. Even being a bystander while

6 *For the Lord knows and is fully acquainted with the way of the righteous, but the way of the ungodly [those living outside God's will] shall perish (end in ruin and come to naught).*

Side Note: Drugabuse.gov and guttmacher.org

1. Nine percent of 8th graders, 23.5 percent of 10th graders, and 37.4 percent of 12th graders reported use of alcohol.
2. Use of illicit drugs for all grades combined was 27.2 percent in 2014 and has risen to 47% in recent years.
3. The reported use of marijuana among 8th graders was at 6.5 percent, among 10th graders at 16.6 percent, and among 12th graders at 21.2 percent.
4. 16% of teens have had sex by age 15, compared with one-third of those aged 16, nearly half (48%) of those aged 17, 61% of 18-year-olds and 71% of 19-year-olds.

Prayer: Father, help me to truly know how blessed I am. I pray that I will dive into your Holy Word so that my roots will grow deep and strong. Be my living water, God, my source of life every moment of every day. I want to be in right standing with you, and I want

sin takes place around us is warned against. The two men who passed by the injured man in the parable of the Good Samaritan, Peter while denying Christ, and those in the crowd while Jesus was being sentenced to death, were just as guilty as the attackers. We are called to love the ungodly and share the truth of the cross with them, but we are not to live among them (John 17:13-18).

We are (here's the "do" list) to enjoy, follow, and obey God's Word. We are to live among His Word, studying and pondering it throughout the day and even at night (vs. 2). Prosperity comes through knowing and following the teachings of God, through obedience and service to Him (Job 36:11). What will happen if we decide to dwell in the Word instead of the world? Verse 3 says we will be like a tree firmly planted and taken care of by streams of water. This water is the Word of God (John 4:14). This water gives life continuously and causes our fruit to develop properly and in the right time.

If we are the tree, then what is the fruit we bear? The fruit is the outer display of our inner choices. Our thoughts eventually lead to words and actions, and these words and actions cause things to manifest in our lives. Continuously staying in the Word instead of the world will change the fruit we bear (Matthew 7 and Galatians 15:19-23).

This water, which is the Word of God, blesses us when we believe it, trust it, and rely on it (Jeremiah 17:7-8). It causes hope and confidence in the Lord. Only when our roots spread deep by the river will we be able to stand tall and strong even when heat comes. Pressures will come in this life that can cause an un-rooted or a shallowly rooted person to become anxious and fearful and wither away.

According to verse 4, those who live in disobedience to God become dead and their lives are without substance. They do not develop roots and are easily blown away when the storms of life come. This is why so many young people turn to drugs, alcohol, and sex (see side note). Their lives have no substance, no meaning because they have no faith, no hope, no living water. They are also without justification

my life to draw others to you. In Jesus name I pray, Amen.

How have you been blessed? Count your blessings here as a reminder of God's faithfulness:

List people you want to come to Christ and pray for them to be drawn to Him by the love and power of the Holy Spirit. Pray He will give you the right words at the right time to be a light to them:

when judgment comes (vs. 5). They don't have a covering because they have not formed a relationship with God. We can see in the natural world how the lives of people like this perish even before they die, but even more disturbing is that their ruin will be eternal if they do not change their hearts.

Verse 6 says that God knows the righteous, those who follow Him; He is fully acquainted with them. However, He is not fully acquainted with the ungodly, those who live outside of His will. His will is His Word, so the ungodly live outside the Word of God. They try to live without water, and it never works. We were designed by the Creator to need water. Physically we would die within 1 week without water. Spiritually, we are also designed to need a relationship with God, which we foster as we drink His living Word.

As we fill our spirits with godly teaching, our lives will begin to overflow and be blessed. Then, as we are blessed, we become a blessing to those around us. We can share our heavenly water with those thirsty souls in our neighborhood, school or on the job. People should be able to see the fruit in our life and eventually want what we have (remember the enviable part from vs. 1). Then they too can begin to delve into the living water of God's Word day and night and put forth deep, strong roots. They will be blessed, and the cycle will continue as they live blessed, prosperous, fortunate, and enviable lives.

Week 1 Day 1 Notes for Psalm 1: Which verse stood out to you the most and why?

_____

_____

_____

_____

What important life lesson can you apply from this Psalm?

_____

_____

_____

_____

Week 1 Day 2 Devotion: Re-read Psalm 1:1-2 and the following verses on living a blessed life.

James 1: 25 *But he who looks carefully into the faultless law, the [law] of liberty, and is faithful to it and perseveres in looking into it, being not a heedless listener who forgets but an active doer [who obeys], he shall be blessed in his doing (his life of obedience).*

Luke 11:28 *But He (Jesus) said, Blessed (happy and to be envied) rather are those who hear the Word of God and obey and practice it!*

Revelation 1:3 *Blessed (happy, prosperous, to be admired) is he who reads and those who hear the words of the prophecy, and who keep the things which are written in it [heeding them and taking them to heart]; for the time [of fulfillment] is near.*

What does it mean to be a "doer" and a "keeper" of God's Word according to James 1 and Revelation 1?

_____

What does the Bible promise to those who obey the Word? _____

List 3 specific things you can do today to be "an active doer" of God's Word.

_____

_____

_____

_____

Week 1 Day 3 Devotion: Re-read Psalm 1:3 and the following verses on being fruitful.

John 15:16 *You have not chosen Me, but I have chosen you and I have appointed and placed and purposefully planted you, so that you would go and bear fruit and keep on bearing, and that your fruit will remain and be lasting, so that whatever you ask of the Father in My name [as My representative] He may give to you.*

Colossians 1:10 *so that you will walk in a manner worthy of the Lord [displaying admirable character, moral courage, and personal integrity], to [fully] please Him in all things, bearing fruit in every good work and steadily growing in the knowledge of God [with deeper faith, clearer insight and fervent love for His precepts];*

Galatians 5:22-23 *But the fruit of the Spirit [the result of His presence within us] is love [unselfish concern for others], joy, [inner] peace, patience [not the ability to wait, but how we act while waiting], kindness, goodness, faithfulness, gentleness, self-control. Against such things there is no law.*

According to John 15, for what reasons does God plant you?

_____

_____

_____

_____

What good fruit do you consistently bear for God?

_____

_____

What additional fruit would you like to bear?

_____

_____

_____

_____

Week 1 Day 4 Devotion: Re-read Psalm 1:3 and the following verses on God as our water source/source of life.

John 4:13-14 _Jesus answered her, "Everyone who drinks this water will be thirsty again. But whoever drinks the water that I give him will never be thirsty again. But the water that I give him will become in him a spring of water [satisfying his thirst for God] welling up [continually flowing, bubbling within him] to eternal life."_

John 7:38 _He who believes in Me [who adheres to, trusts in, and relies on Me], as the Scripture has said, 'From his innermost being will flow continually rivers of living water.'"_

Isaiah 12:3 _Therefore with joy you will draw water from the springs of salvation._

Why is salvation compared to flowing water?

_____

_____

How can that "water" change your life here on Earth?

_____

_____

Week 1 Day 5 Devotion: Re-read Psalm 1:4 and the following verses on wickedness.

Ephesians 5:11-12 *Do not participate in the worthless and unproductive deeds of darkness, but instead expose them [by exemplifying personal integrity, moral courage, and godly character]; for it is disgraceful even to mention the things that such people practice in secret.*

Proverbs 24:1-2 *Do not be envious of evil men, Nor desire to be with them; For their minds plot violence, And their lips talk of trouble [for the innocent].*

Proverbs 4:14-15 *Do not enter the path of the wicked, And do not go the way of evil men. Avoid it, do not travel on it; Turn away from it and pass on.*

Most people do not view themselves as wicked, but wickedness is sin and we have all sinned. Ephesians 5 tells us not to participate in darkness but to expose it. We expose it by:

_____

_____

Proverbs 4 warns against not traveling the way of or with evil men. Name one sin you committed because you were influenced by someone around you?

_____

_____

_____

How can you avoid this kind of situation in the future?

_____

_____

_____

_____

Week 1 Day 6 Devotions: Re-read Psalm 1:5-6 and the following verses on what happens to the wicked vs. the righteous.

Proverbs 4:18 *But the path of the just (righteous) is like the light of dawn, that shines brighter and brighter until [it reaches its full strength and glory in] the perfect day.*

Proverbs 10:2-3 *Treasures of wickedness and ill-gotten gains do not profit, but righteousness and moral integrity in daily life rescues from death. The Lord will not allow the righteous to hunger [God will meet all his needs], But He will reject and cast away the craving of the wicked.*

Revelation 21:8 But *as for the cowards and unbelieving and abominable [who are devoid of character and personal integrity and practice or tolerate immorality], and murderers, and sorcerers [with intoxicating drugs], and idolaters and occultists [who practice and teach false religions], and all the liars [who knowingly deceive and twist truth], their part will be in the lake that blazes with fire and brimstone, which is the second death."*

According to these verses, what will happen to the wicked?

_____

_____

What will happen to the righteous?

_____

_____

How does seeing the contrast of what will happen to the wicked (unsaved, unrepentant sinner) vs. the righteous (a redeemed by the blood sinner) encourage you to live right and witness to those around you?

_____

_____

_____

_____

Week 1 Day 7 Devotions: Re-read Psalm 1:6 and the following verses on God knowing you.

Psalm 139: 1-3 *O Lord, you have searched me [thoroughly] and have known me. You know when I sit down and when I rise up [my entire life, everything I do]; You understand my thought from afar. You scrutinize my path and my lying down, and You are intimately acquainted with all my ways.*

John 10:14-15 *I am the Good Shepherd, and I know [without any doubt those who are] My own and My own know Me [and have a deep, personal relationship with Me]— even as the Father knows Me and I know the Father—and I lay down My [very own] life [sacrificing it] for the benefit of the sheep.*

1 Peter 3:12 *For the eyes of the Lord are [looking favorably] upon the righteous (the upright), And His ears are attentive to their prayer (eager to answer), But the face of the Lord is against those who practice evil."*

How does the fact that God knows you, sees you, and hears you make you feel?

_____

_____

_____

How does the fact that Jesus knows all of your faults and mistakes and still chose to die for you make you feel?

_____

_____

_____

How do these facts affect the way you live your life?

_____

_____

_____

Week 2 Day 1: Psalm 2

¹ Why do the nations assemble with commotion [uproar and confusion of voices], and why do the people imagine (meditate upon and devise) an empty scheme?
² The kings of the earth take their places; the rulers take counsel together against the Lord and His Anointed One (the Messiah, the Christ). They say,
³ Let us break Their bands [of restraint] asunder and cast Their cords [of control] from us.
⁴ He Who sits in the heavens laughs; the Lord has them in derision [and in supreme contempt He mocks them].
⁵ He speaks to them in His deep anger and troubles (terrifies and confounds) them in His displeasure and fury, saying,
⁶ Yet have I anointed (installed and placed) My King [firmly] on My holy hill of Zion.
⁷ I will declare the decree of the Lord: He said to Me, You are My Son; this day [I declare] I have begotten You.
⁸ Ask of Me, and I will give You the nations as Your inheritance, and the uttermost parts of the earth as Your possession.
⁹ You shall break them with a rod of iron; You shall dash them in pieces like potters' ware.

You may not know that some of the chapters in Psalms contain prophecy. Prophetic words in the Bible are special insights that God gave to the person speaking or writing them– a prophet (Numbers 12:6). We still have prophets today (1 Corinthians 12:10, 14:3). This is not the same thing as fortune telling. Fortune-telling involves the use of demonic spirits to tell a person's future and includes horoscopes, tarot cards, palm reading, Ouija boards etc. The Bible warns against being involved in such practices (Leviticus 20:6, 2 Peter 2:1-3). Prophecies in the Bible serve a greater purpose and come from the Holy Spirit, who is part of God (2 Peter 1:21). God revealed certain future events in special circumstances to either encourage the Israelites or to warn them. We too are to learn the lessons the Israelites learned.

This chapter in Psalms prophetically speaks of the coming Christ, as well as the scheming of nations who would come against Jesus. In verse 1 we see nations coming together in an uproar. There are so many voices that it causes confusion. What are the voices saying? They are saying what they have been thinking- remember we talked about meditating in chapter 1. What you meditate on will manifest eventually and will affect your life and the lives of others. In this chapter, rulers have been meditating on empty schemes. The rulers have come together to discuss their opposition to the Lord (God) and His Anointed One (Jesus) (vs. 2). The rulers say out loud, "Let us break away from God the Father, God the Son, and God the Holy Spirit! They cannot control us anymore!"

Wow! It takes a lot of nerve and foolishness to say that kind of thing, but isn't that exactly what nations have done for centuries? Isn't that what nations around the world, and even our own United States, are doing right now? When leaders create laws that go against biblical principles, they are scheming against God. The Old Testament is filled with nations who basically said the same thing and came against God's chosen people, the Israelites. Time and time again

10 Now therefore, O you kings, act wisely; be instructed and warned, O you rulers of the earth.
11 Serve the Lord with reverent awe and worshipful fear; rejoice and be in high spirits with trembling [lest you displease Him].
12 Kiss the Son [pay homage to Him in purity], lest He be angry and you perish in the way, for soon shall His wrath be kindled. O blessed (happy, fortunate, and to be envied) are all those who seek refuge and put their trust in Him!

Side Note:

accordingtothescriptures.org and ibisworld.com

1. It is said that over 300 prophecies were fulfilled at Jesus' birth, death, and resurrection.
2. Almost 2 billion dollars is spent on fortune telling/ psychics per year in America.

Prayer: Father, forgive me for my empty schemes and for any time I have gone against your will, which is the Word of God. Thank you for sending your son, Jesus, to die on the cross for my sins. I repent for my sins and for my nation's leaders who have gone against You as well. Forgive our leaders and change their hearts, that they would serve you, Lord. I love you and

God crushed the opposition, and He will again when He returns after the Tribulation.

Verses 4 and 5 paint a picture of God sitting in the heavens looking down at these puny rulers with contempt toward their attitudes. His voice booms out and He speaks to them. What does the God of the universe say to these ungodly people? He tells them that He has placed Jesus as king. He decrees or declares that Jesus is His begotten son (vs. 6,7). He gives the nations to Jesus and a prophecy of destruction is given (vs. 8,9).

Now, before you start to picture God as a larger-than-life angry bully, you must keep reading. In the final three verses of Psalm 2, we see that the kings of the nations have now been warned. They have been clearly taught what will happen if they continue to come against God. Every good parent should clearly define what is expected of their children, as well as the consequences of wrong behavior. This is not only fair but loving. For example, it would not be proper for parents to punish a child for stealing if the child was never taught it was wrong. Likewise, it would not be fair to dole out random punishments for misbehavior when the child did not fully understand the consequences.

God our father loves us so much that He himself declared His love by sending Jesus to die for our sins. He decrees His will and explains His expectations to us throughout the Bible because He is a good parent. In this Psalm He tells the nations, past, present, and future that if they will serve Him then He will be happy with them. They will be blessed if they will put their trust in Him (vs. 12). However, if they do not revere and joyfully worship Him, then He will become angry and they will perish.

This lesson to the nations' rulers is also a lesson for all people. God formally and officially foretold the coming of Jesus. He issued the decree over 1,000 years before Jesus' birth. We can trust that His decrees, His Word is true (Acts 3:18). God is not a liar; therefore, we can have faith in His Word (Numbers 23:19, Titus 1:2). We are to serve Him like He commanded the kings. We too can speak His word out

worship you. I seek your refuge and put my trust in You fully. In Jesus' name, Amen

loud, instead of rebellious words like the kings of the earth did in verse 2. As we speak His words out of our mouth and have faith in those words, we will see God move. As we make Him our refuge and put our trust in Him, we will be blessed (vs. 12).

Week 2 Day 1 Notes for Psalm 2: Which verse stood out to you the most and why?

_____

_____

_____

_____

What important life lesson can you apply from this Psalm?

_____

_____

_____

_____

Week 2 Day 2 Devotions: Re-read Psalm 2:1-3 and the following verses on rebellion.

Ezekiel 12:2-3 *"Son of man, you live among a rebellious house, who have eyes to see but do not see, who have ears to hear but do not hear; for they are a rebellious people.*

1 Samuel 15:22-23 *"For rebellion is as [serious as] the sin of divination (fortune-telling), and disobedience is as [serious as] false religion and idolatry. Because you have rejected the word of the Lord, He also has rejected you as king."*

Hebrews 3:15 *…while it is said, "Today [while there is still opportunity] if you hear His voice, Do not harden your heart, as when they provoked Me [in the rebellion in the desert at Meribah]."*

In what ways do you see rebellion, disobedience, or hard hearts in the world today?

_____

_____

_____

_____

How can you have "eyes to see" and "ears to hear" in a world of people who rebel against God?

_____

_____

_____

_____

Week 2 Day 3 Devotions: Re-read Psalm 2: 4-5 and the following verses on how God responds to rebellion.

1 Samuel 12:14-15 *If you will fear the Lord [with awe and profound reverence] and serve Him and listen to His voice and not rebel against His commandment, then both you and your king will follow the Lord your God [and it will be well]. But if you do not listen to the Lord's voice, but rebel against His command, then the hand of the Lord will be against you [to punish you], as it was against your fathers.*

Isaiah 65:2-3 *"I have spread out My hands all the day long to a rebellious and stubborn people, who walk in the way that is not good, [following] after their own thoughts and intentions, The people who continually provoke Me to My face, Sacrificing [to idols] in gardens and making offerings with incense on bricks [instead of at the designated altar];*

Nehemiah 9:28 *"But as soon as they had rest, they again did evil before You; therefore You abandoned them into the hand of their enemies, so that they ruled over them. Yet when they turned and cried out again to You, You heard them from heaven, And You rescued them many times in accordance with Your compassion,*

All will be well for those who fear the Lord and serve Him, but those who rebel will be punished. What character traits do you see in God in Is. 65 and Neh. 9 despite consistent rebellion?

_____

_____

_____

_____

How can you use that to win someone to God?

_____

_____

_____

_____

Week 2 Day 4 Devotions: Re-read Psalm 2: 6-8 and the following verses on how God sent Jesus to rule the nations.

Revelation 2:27 [and] *he shall shepherd and rule them with a rod of iron, as the earthen pots are broken in pieces, as I also have received authority [and power to rule them] from My Father;*

Luke 1:30-33 *The angel said to her, "Do not be afraid, Mary, for you have found favor with God. Listen carefully: you will conceive in your womb and give birth to a son, and you shall name Him Jesus. He will be great and eminent and will be called the Son of the Most High; and the Lord God will give Him the throne of His father David; and He will reign over the house of Jacob (Israel) forever, and of His kingdom there shall be no end."*

Isaiah 9:6 *For to us a Child shall be born, to us a Son shall be given; And the government shall be upon His shoulder, and His name shall be called Wonderful Counselor, Mighty God, Everlasting Father, Prince of Peace.*

What does knowing Jesus will reign over all one day mean to you?

_____

_____

_____

_____

Week 2 Day 5 Devotions: Re-read Psalm 2: 10 and the following verses on wisdom.

Ephesians 5:15-16 *Therefore see that you walk carefully [living life with honor, purpose, and courage; shunning those who tolerate and enable evil], not as the unwise, but as wise [sensible, intelligent, discerning people], making the very most of your time [on earth, recognizing and taking advantage of each opportunity and using it with wisdom and diligence], because the days are [filled with] evil.*

James 1:5 *If any of you lacks wisdom [to guide him through a decision or circumstance], he is to ask of [our benevolent] God, who gives to everyone generously and without rebuke or blame, and it will be given to him.*

James 3:17 *But the wisdom from above is first pure [morally and spiritually undefiled], then peace-loving [courteous, considerate], gentle, reasonable [and willing to listen], full of compassion and good fruits. It is unwavering, without [self-righteous] hypocrisy [and self-serving guile].*

How does a wise person act according to these verses?

_____

_____

_____

Which of these characteristics do you want to exhibit most in your life?

_____

_____

_____

_____

Week 2 Day 6 Devotions: Re-read Psalm 2: 11 and the following verses on the fear of the Lord.

Proverbs 1:7 *The [reverent] fear of the Lord [that is, worshiping Him and regarding Him as truly awesome] is the beginning and the preeminent part of knowledge [its starting point and its essence];*

Psalm 128:1-2 *Blessed [happy and sheltered by God's favor] is everyone who fears the Lord [and worships Him with obedience], Who walks in His ways and lives according to His commandments. For you shall eat the fruit of [the labor of] your hands, You will be happy and blessed and it will be well with you.*

Luke 1:50 *"And His mercy is upon generation after generation toward those who [stand in great awe of God and] fear Him. From generation to generation.*

What benefits will you receive when you live in reverent fear of the Lord?

_____

_____

Who can you share this knowledge with that does not fear the Lord?

_____

_____

Week 2 Day 7 Devotions: Re-read Psalm 2: 12 and the following verses on putting your trust in the Lord.

Proverbs 3:5-6 *Trust in and rely confidently on the Lord with all your heart and do not rely on your own insight or understanding. In all your ways know and acknowledge and recognize Him, And He will make your paths straight and smooth [removing obstacles that block your way].*

Romans 15:13 NIV *May the God of hope fill you with all joy and peace as you trust in him, so that you may overflow with hope by the power of the Holy Spirit.*

Jeremiah 17:7-8 *"Blessed [with spiritual security] is the man who believes and trusts in and relies on the Lord And whose hope and confident expectation is the Lord.*

What benefits follow when you put your trust in God?

_____

_____

_____

_____

Write down at least one area of your life where you need to trust Him more.

_____

_____

_____

_____

Week 3 Day 1: Psalm 3

A Psalm of David. When he fled from Absalom his son.

¹ Lord, how they are increased who trouble me! Many are they who rise up against me.
² Many are saying of me, there is no help for him in God. Selah [pause, and calmly think of that]!
³ But You, O Lord, are a shield for me, my glory, and the lifter of my head.
⁴ With my voice I cry to the Lord, and He hears and answers me out of His holy hill. Selah [pause, and calmly think of that]!
⁵ I lay down and slept; I wakened again, for the Lord sustains me.
⁶ I will not be afraid of ten thousands of people who have set themselves against me round about.
⁷ Arise, O Lord; save me, O my God! For You have struck all my enemies on the cheek; You have broken the teeth of the ungodly.
⁸ Salvation belongs to the Lord; May Your blessing be upon Your people. Selah [pause, and calmly think of that]!

Shield Reference:
christdeaf.org and **bible-archaeology.info**

Side Note: Usatoday.com, npr.org, and ncbi.nlm.nih.gov

1. There's a suicide in the USA every 13 minutes and over 40,000 annually.

David's very own son, Absalom, had turned against him. His flesh and blood was out for blood. Can you imagine someone you have loved with your whole heart turning against you to kill you? Maybe you have not experienced such an extreme form of betrayal, but unfortunately many of us have been hurt by someone we loved and trusted. I know I have felt the pangs of this very topic. Some members of my family turned against me in a very serious way and caused damage that cannot be explained with words. As I was walking through the storm they created, I relied on the Psalms to comfort and teach me. I could easily relate to David's anguish and confusion as time and time again he was sought after by Saul and others (vs. 1)

People were even telling David that God couldn't or wouldn't help him (vs.2) How tragic the situation becomes when we feel that we are beyond God's help. How tragic it is when those around us have no comfort for us. That is the very place where people are often pushed to the brink of suicide, when they feel there is no hope, and they have no support (see side note p. 16). Thankfully that was not the case for me. I had many encouragers in my life who lifted me up and told me that God was at work even though I couldn't see it yet.

My tears would fall to the page as I read David's pleadings because the pain was so real for him and for me, but it comforted me somehow to know that I wasn't the only one to suffer great hurt by someone I loved. It comforted me to see David lift up his head and trust God to get him through yet another crisis. Yes, David was downcast and downright depressed and afraid for his life, but in verse 3 he says something profound – "but You, Oh Lord!" "I am afraid, but You..." "I am betrayed, but You…" "I'm sad, but You..." "I'm angry, but You..." "You, O Lord, are my shield. You cover me completely from anything that comes at me!"

In ancient times, before the Romans and Greeks conquered the world, you might be surprised to know that a shield used in battle was not the typical small round shield

2. Nearly 60 million Americans are affected by a sleep disorder.
3. Depression and anxiety are 2 common factors in insomnia.

Prayer: Hear me oh, Father. I call out to you because I am in need of your protection, encouragement, rest… (list your own personal needs here):

You are a true and faithful God. I trust you. You have defeated my enemies and lift me out of fear, depression, anger… (list your own specific needs here):

You are my salvation. I praise you and ask you to bless all your people. Amen

portrayed in paintings and on statues. Round shields were mainly to protect the soldiers face in hand-to-hand combat. Some were used for sparring, while others were decorative and used for ceremonies. So, what did a typical war shield look like back in the time of David, you might wonder? They were nearly as tall as a door! In fact, some shields were measured to fit the person it was designed to protect. Many were made of wood or with reeds tightly woven together and were covered in animal skin. The shield was designed to protect the entire body of the soldier.

Arrows were one of the main weapons used in biblical warfare. Some enemies would light the tip of the arrow on fire, thus the need for a large protective shield versus the small round shield. This information is pertinent considering what David says about God being His shield in verse 3. God completely covered David and protected him from everything coming at him from the front. This same picture is painted for us in Ephesians 6:16 when Paul tells us to "…take up the shield of faith, with which you can extinguish all the flaming arrows of the evil one." God knows you. He knows your measurements, your need, and He fits you with Himself in the very measurement of who you are and the circumstance you face. That thought touches the core of my heart as I type the words. It makes me pause in awe of His love and grace toward us. His very glory, everything He is covers me. Selah, pause and calmly think of that!

God is our shield, but He also gives us spiritual weapons to protect ourselves. Satan shoots flaming arrows in the form of thoughts, words, temptations and circumstances that he uses to try to defeat us. He comes when we are at our weakest to exploit our weaknesses. If we doubt God's Word, our shield of faith goes down and leaves us defenseless. That is the place where David finds himself many times throughout the Psalms, and sometimes he has caused the problem himself. However, in Psalm 3 it is not due to fault of his own but because his son is hunting him like a dog.

We have discussed so much and are just getting to the second half of verse 3! I bet you didn't realize how much such a tiny chapter in the Bible could teach you! I know that I have been guilty of reading through my devotions so quickly that I miss what depth God has in store for me. That is partly why I began writing this Bible study in the first place.

The second lesson in verse 3 involves the word glory. I would like to briefly explain the significance of this to you now. David is saying here that God is his glory, his rear guard. He is saying, "You have my back, God!" The glory represents God's abiding presence in our lives. This was visible as a cloud by day and a pillar of fire by night to the Israelites as they traveled in the wilderness to reclaim their land (Exodus 14: 19,20). In Isaiah 58:8, Isaiah says that the glory of the Lord will be our rear guard. Isaiah 52:12 says that God will go before us and be our rear guard. So, God is not only our shield protecting us from the front, but He is also protecting us from behind. It is no wonder that David called out to God and trusted him to do something mighty on his behalf in verse 4. David knows that when we can barely hold our head up from weariness, worry, and depression, when we are surrounded on all sides by evil or temptation, He will protect us and lift our head for us. David had no other choice but to fully believe that God heard him and would answer his plea, lest he give up and die.

What happens next should amaze you! He slept! Millions of people suffer from depression or stress related insomnia each year (see side note). I know that when our family was in the midst of the crisis I could not sleep through the night. I would toss and turn, doze for a little while, lay awake for a while, and the cycle would repeat itself a dozen times until the sun peeked through the window. I would pray continuously but my heart was afraid. I would cry out in the middle of the night for relief and rescue. While we were not miraculously delivered from a horrible situation, God did sustain us (vs. 5). He gave us the chance and the strength to face another day. People and circumstances had "set themselves against" us (vs. 6), and though they weren't out for blood, our lives would never be the same because of their deceit and treachery. We had seen God do many things in our past just as David had, so we decided to trust Him.

David recalls in verse 7 that God had already defeated enemies for him. In fact, he basically says that God punched them in the face and knocked out their teeth like a heavyweight boxing champion! He knew from his past that God could and would protect him. He knew what the people said in verse 2 was not true. Be careful who you listen to, especially in a crisis. Satan will come at you hard with his fiery arrows and get others to work on his behalf to defeat you. Listen to godly counsel when you're in trouble. Get into the Word to find encouragement and answers. Be wary of the lies your emotions will tell you; salvation belongs to the Lord! (vs. 8)

There's one final thing to note about the end of Psalm 3. David turns from his inward struggle to God. Then in verse 8 he turns his thoughts from a personal prayer and personal encouragement to his people. He calls for a blessing upon his nation, the nation of Israel. He acknowledges that God will sustain and protect anyone who belongs to him. God is no respecter of persons (Acts 10:34). His shield and glory are for all who put their trust in Him. His salvation is for all who dare to look upward from their pit and sin and cry out to Him for mercy. "I was a drug addict, but God…" "I was a murderer, but God…" "I was an adulterer, but God…" "I was_____but God…"

Billions of people across this world and throughout the pages of time have a "but God" testimony. If you don't, you can right now. You don't need a fancy or formal prayer. Just call out to Him for salvation if that is your need. Call out to Him for healing if that is your need. Call out to Him for a lost loved one. Whatever the need is, call to God in faith just as David did and then rest. Rest your mind and body knowing that God sustains you (vs. 5) and that He has already given the enemy a 1, 2 knockout punch for you! Selah, pause and calmly think of that!

Week 3 Day 1 Notes for Psalm 3: Which verse stood out to you the most and why?

_____

_____

_____

_____

What important life lesson can you apply from this Psalm?

_____

_____

Week 3 Day 2 Devotions: Re-read Psalm 3:1-2 and the following verses on trouble/enemies rising against us.

Psalm 37:1-2 *Do not worry because of evildoers, nor be envious toward wrongdoers; For they will wither quickly like the grass, And fade like the green herb.*

Exodus 23:22 *But if you will indeed listen to and truly obey His voice and do everything that I say, then I will be an enemy to your enemies and an adversary to your adversaries.*

John 16:33 [1] *have told you these things, so that in Me you may have [perfect] peace. In the world you have tribulation and distress and suffering, but be courageous [be confident, be undaunted, be filled with joy]; I have overcome the world." [My conquest is accomplished, My victory abiding.]*

What can you count on happening to enemies and troubled times when they arise in your life?

_____

_____

How does your answer to the question above give you courage as defined in John 16:33?

_____

_____

_____

Week 3 Day 3 Devotions: Re-read Psalm 3:3 and the following verses on God as our shield.

Deuteronomy 33:29 *"Happy and blessed are you, O Israel; Who is like you, a people saved by the Lord, The Shield of your help, And the Sword of your majesty! Your enemies will cringe before you, and you will tread on their high places [tramping down their idolatrous altars]."*

Proverbs 30:5 *Every word of God is tested and refined [like silver]; He is a shield to those who trust and take refuge in Him.*

Psalm 28:7 *The Lord is my strength and my [impenetrable] shield; My heart trusts [with unwavering confidence] in Him, and I am helped; therefore my heart greatly rejoices,*

What do you have to do in order for God to be your shield according to Proverbs 30?

_____

_____

_____

What do Deuteronomy 33 and Psalm 28 say is the result of Him becoming your shield?

_____

_____

_____

Week 3 Day 4 Devotions: Re-read Psalm 3:4 and the following verses on God answering prayers.

Matthew 7:7 *Ask and keep on asking and it will be given to you; seek and keep on seeking and you will find; knock and keep on knocking and the door will be opened to you.*

Mark 11:24 *For this reason I am telling you, whatever things you ask for in prayer [in accordance with God's will], believe [with confident trust] that you have received them, and they will be given to you.*

John 14:13-14 *And I will do whatever you ask in My name as My representative], this I will do, so that the Father may be glorified and celebrated in the Son. If you ask Me anything in My name [as My representative], I will do it.*

What are the prerequisites (actions required of you) in these verses for you to be confident that God will answer your prayers?

_____

_____

_____

What does knowing that God answers your prayers mean to you?

_____

_____

_____

Week 3 Day 5 Devotions: Re-read Psalm 3:5 and the following verses on God sustaining us—strengthening or supporting us mentally or physically.

Isaiah 41:13 *"For I the Lord your God keep hold of your right hand; [I am the Lord], Who says to you, 'Do not fear, I will help you.'*

Deuteronomy 1:31 *and in the wilderness where you saw how the Lord your God carried and protected you, just as a man carries his son, all along the way which you traveled until you arrived at this place.'*

Philippians 4:13[1] *can do all things [which He has called me to do] through Him who strengthens and empowers me [to fulfill His purpose—I am self-sufficient in Christ's sufficiency; I am ready for anything and equal to anything through Him who infuses me with inner strength and confident peace.]*

According to Isaiah and Deuteronomy, what 5 things will God do for you (look at His actions)?

_____

_____

_____

What then is your response to those actions, according to Philippians 4?

_____

_____

_____

_____

Week 3 Day 6 Devotions: Re-read Psalm 3:6 and the following verses on not being afraid.

Psalm 118:6 *The Lord is on my side; I will not fear. What can [mere] man do to me?*

2 Timothy 1:7 *For God did not give us a spirit of timidity or cowardice or fear, but [He has given us a spirit] of power and of love and of sound judgment and personal discipline [abilities that result in a calm, well-balanced mind and self-control].*

Deuteronomy 31:6 ^{Be} *strong and courageous, do not be afraid or tremble in dread before them, for it is the Lord your God who goes with you. He will not fail you or abandon you."*

According to these verses, what character traits are the opposite of fear?

_____

_____

_____

According to these verses, why should you not be afraid?

_____

_____

_____

Week 3 Day 7 Devotions: Re-read Psalm 3:6 and the following verses on victory.

1 Corinthians 15:56-57 *The sting of death is sin, and the power of sin [by which it brings death] is the law;* ⁵⁷ *but thanks be to God, who gives us the victory [as conquerors] through our Lord Jesus Christ.*

2 Corinthians 2:14 *But thanks be to God, who always leads us in triumph in Christ, and through us spreads and makes evident everywhere the sweet fragrance of the knowledge of Him.*

1 John 5:4 *For everyone born of God is victorious and overcomes the world; and this is the victory that has conquered and overcome the world—our [continuing, persistent] faith [in Jesus the Son of God].*

How do you get victory?

_____

_____

_____

_____

What do you have victory over?

_____

_____

_____

_____

According to 2 Corinthians, what is the purpose of your victory?

_____

_____

_____

_____

Week 4 Day 1: Psalm 4

¹ Answer me when I call, O God of my righteousness (uprightness, justice, and right standing with You)! You have freed me when I was hemmed in and enlarged me when I was in distress; have mercy upon me and hear my prayer. ² O you sons of men, how long will you turn my honor and glory into shame? How long will you love vanity and futility and seek after lies? Selah [pause, and calmly think of that]! ³ But know that the Lord has set apart for Himself [and given distinction to] him who is godly [the man of loving-kindness]. The Lord listens and heeds when I call to Him. ⁴ Be angry [or stand in awe] and sin not; commune with your own hearts upon your beds and be silent (sorry for the things you say in your hearts). Selah [pause, and calmly think of that]! ⁵ Offer just and right sacrifices; trust (lean on and be confident) in the Lord. ⁶ Many say, Oh, that we might see some good! Lift up the light of Your countenance upon us, O Lord. ⁷ You have put more joy and rejoicing in my heart than [they know] when their wheat and new wine have yielded abundantly.

Once again David is calling for God to answer his prayer (vs. 1). He is not doing this disrespectfully or begging out of doubt. It is more like a declaration that God will have mercy on him and answer him. He says that God is his righteousness and that he has been freed from a time when he was hemmed in and enlarged when he was in distress (vs. 1). The latter part of this verse means that David has been led out of trouble into open and prosperous places.

I would like to focus on the first part of this verse for a few moments—righteousness. Righteousness is an important topic to discuss and vital for a believer to understand. We need to know who we are in Christ so that we can feel assured of our heavenly status and confident when we come to God for answers. It's hard to think of ourselves as being righteous. After all, our righteousness is as filthy rags (Isaiah 64:6) compared to God's righteousness, and we are often reminded of how wretched we are: "Amazing grace how sweet the sound that saved a wretch like me..." God is righteous; we know that from Deuteronomy 32:4, so how in the world can David or any of us say that we are righteous? Let's look at some scriptures to clarify this point.

Romans 3:20-24 basically tells us that we are sinners and are unrighteous. We could never be righteous just by following the laws set forth in the Old Testament because no one could uphold them 100%. Our righteousness (justification, clearing of wrongdoing, and right standing with God) only comes through Jesus. We do nothing to deserve it or earn it. Our successes and failures cannot affect it. Romans 3:25 from The Message says, "God sacrificed Jesus on the altar of the world to clear that world of sin. Having faith in him sets us in the clear." 2 Corinthians 5:21 says, "For our sake He made Christ [virtually] to be sin Who knew no sin, so that in *and* through Him we might become [endued with, viewed as being in, and examples of] the righteousness of God [what we ought to be, approved and acceptable and in right relationship with Him, by His goodness]."

Without accepting that God has made us righteous, we can never truly be set free from our sins. Without this

⁸ In peace I will both lie down and sleep, for You, Lord, alone make me dwell in safety and confident trust.

Side Note:

God shows mercy even after wicked people anger Him. He warned even the vilest people groups of His anger with their sin so that they had an opportunity to repent and not receive His righteous wrath. If they repented, then He honored His promise not to make them face the consequences of sin. If they did not repent, then He followed through on the punishment. Pride, rebellion, and deception are what keep people from repentance.

1. He sent Jonah to Nineveh to preach repentance. The people repented and were saved.
2. He had Noah preach repentance to the people for 100 years while he built the ark so that they could be saved, unfortunately only his family listened.
3. He was going to spare Sodom and Gomorrah if 10 people were found to be righteous, but none could be found because they were too deep in sin and were blinded by their evil ways.
   However, Lot and his family were saved.

knowledge and acceptance of what Christ has done for us and who we are in Christ, we have a hard time standing on God's promises and expecting to see His action on our behalf. We can expect God's action because of His righteousness and the honoring of His promises to us from the Bible. Since we have established that we are the righteousness of God through Christ, we know that this entitles us to eternal redemption. Because of this, we like David, are free from what hems us in too. God hears our prayer, and we receive God's mercy (vs. 1)

David moves on in verse 2 to question why ungodly men have tried to dishonor him. He questions their motives and says that they love themselves too much and seek after lies. I believe, in this case, lies may be what these prideful men are searching for, not only to discredit David and his righteousness through God but also to make themselves look good. When people allow pride into their hearts, they usually allow themselves to be deceived and they deceive others. Jealousy rises up from a pride filled heart and lies to bring others down. This is no way to live and usually brings with it self-destruction.

David is sure that God himself has set godly men apart and listens to them (vs. 3). The verse says that "He heeds when I call." Heed means to pay careful attention to and take interest in. How wonderful it is to know that God pays careful attention to us when we call on Him! In verse 4, he calls for the men from verse 2 not to sin even if they become angry. Now, I believe that in this case these men do not have a valid reason to be angry with David. Pride and jealousy have caused these men to become unrightfully angry with David (If only they could be happy that God has made David righteous. If only they knew they could be righteous too!). He goes on in verse 4 to tell them to be sorry for the things they say in their hearts when they are alone at night. Be assured that God knows our hearts (Jeremiah 17:10).

There is another side to this verse, however. Sometimes we have a right to be angry. When an injustice has been done, someone has hurt us, or someone has sinned, it produces what some call righteous anger. We cannot control what thoughts and emotions pop up inside of us; however, we

4. He spared Rahab when He gave Jericho to the Israelites.

Side Note: psychcentral.com and news.bbc.co.uk

1. 2 out of 8 men have uncontrolled anger issues
2. "Chronic and intense anger has been linked to heart disease, cancer, stroke, colds and flu as well as depression, self-harm and substance misuse. And anger is more likely to have a negative effect on relationships than any other emotion."

Prayer: Thank you, God, for sending Jesus to take away my sins and make me righteous. I know that I have done nothing to deserve this wonderful gift, and nothing can take it away. Thank you for hearing me when I call on you. I pray that you will forgive me for any pride or anger that I have allowed in my heart. I thank you for setting me apart. Shine on me now and let me see your goodness. Fill my heart with joy and peace. Thank you for restful sleep. I trust in you, lean on you, and rely on you completely. Amen

can actively choose not to hold onto those things if they're in disobedience to the Word. Anger may be justified or "righteous" in our minds, but we are not to sin because of it. We are not to say or do something wrong because of that anger. We are not to hold onto the anger because that is sin too and can cause harm (see side note).

God was often angry with Israelites in the Old Testament and with nations who came against them, but this was not because He is mean and wrath filled. He only became angry when they blatantly disobeyed His commands over and over and over again (Ezra 8:22). Jesus was also angered in the New Testament by the attitude of the Pharisees (Mark 3:5). These are considered examples of righteous anger. Remember too that God always gave the Israelites many chances and warnings before He brought about a consequence, and often He spared them due to His great love and mercy. He even spared the Israelite's enemies on several occasions out of mercy or because of their repentance (2 Kings 6:17-25).

Verse 5 tells us to offer just and righteous right sacrifices, sacrifices that are pure and come from the heart. We are also to trust God fully. I like how the amplified Bible explains trust as leaning on and being completely confident in God. Because we can lean on God like this, we will see His goodness (vs. 6). Because He shines His holy light upon us, we have more joy in our hearts than a farmer knows when yielding an abundant harvest (vs. 7). If you have ever planted anything and have taken care of it consistently, then you know what it feels like to see it bloom and produce fruit. As an amateur gardener myself who married into a farming family, I know how much effort goes into a crop. The satisfaction, joy, and relief that accompanies the harvest is intense.

Finally, we again see that as David has reflected on his confidence in God and on God's goodness, he will be able to sleep well. I encourage you to do the same thing before you lie your head down to sleep each night. Think about how God has made you righteous through Christ's sacrifice on the cross. Meditate on his goodness and rejoice! Dwell in His divine safety and rest in confident trust in Him.

Week 4 Day 1 Notes for Psalm 4: Which verse stood out to you the most and why?

_____

_____

_____

What important life lesson can you apply from this Psalm?

_____

_____

_____

Week 4 Day 2 Devotions: Re-read Psalm 4:1 and the following verses on mercy.

Psalm 86:5 _For You, O Lord, are good, and ready to forgive [our sins, sending them away, completely letting them go forever and ever]; And abundant in loving kindness and overflowing in mercy to all those who call upon You._

Hebrews 4:16 _Therefore let us [with privilege] approach the throne of grace [that is, the throne of God's gracious favor] with confidence and without fear, so that we may receive mercy [for our failures] and find [His amazing] grace to help in time of need [an appropriate blessing, coming just at the right moment]._

Ephesians 2:4 _But God, being [so very] rich in mercy, because of His great and wonderful love with which He loved us,_

In Psalm 86, what does God's mercy do to our sin?

_____

_____

How are we to approach the throne of grace in Hebrews?

_____

_____

Remind yourself now of a specific time, besides your salvation if you can, when you received God's mercy in a situation. What was the experience?

_____

_____

How has that experience given you confidence in God?

_____

_____

_____

Week 4 Day 3 Devotions: Re-read Psalm 4:2 and the following verses on vanity (empty pleasure, fruitless desires) and lying.

2 Peter 2:18 *For uttering arrogant words of vanity [pompous words disguised to sound scholarly or profound, but meaning nothing and containing no spiritual truth], they beguile and lure using lustful desires, by sensuality, those who barely escape from the ones who live in error.*

Job 15:31 *"Let him not trust in vanity (emptiness, futility) and be led astray; For emptiness will be his reward [for such living].*

Proverbs 6:16-19 *These six things the Lord hates; Indeed, seven are repulsive to Him: A proud look [the attitude that makes one overestimate oneself and discount others], a lying tongue, and hands that shed innocent blood, A heart that creates wicked plans, Feet that run swiftly to evil, A false witness who breathes out lies [even half-truths], And one who spreads discord (rumors) among brothers.*

Vanity and lies start in your thoughts but end up in your mouth. What is God's reaction to vanity and lies?

_____

_____

What can you do today to guard your thoughts and mouth against these two things?

_____

_____

Week 4 Day 4 Devotions: Re-read Psalm 4:3 and the following verses on being set apart.

2 Corinthians 6:17 *"So come out from among unbelievers and be separate," says the Lord, "And do not touch what is unclean; and I will graciously receive you and welcome you [with favor],*

1 Peter 2:9 ᴮᵘᵗ *you are a chosen race, a royal priesthood, a consecrated nation, a [special] people for God's own possession, so that you may proclaim the excellencies [the wonderful deeds and virtues and perfections] of Him who called you out of darkness into His marvelous light.*

2 Timothy 2:21 *Therefore, if anyone cleanses himself from these things [which are dishonorable—disobedient, sinful], he will be a vessel for honor, sanctified [set apart for a special purpose and], useful to the Master, prepared for every good work.*

What benefits do you receive from being set apart?

_____

_____

_____

According to 1 Peter and 2 Timothy, why does God want us to be set apart?

_____   _____

_____

Week 4 Day 5 Devotions: Re-read Psalm 4:4 and the following verses on being sorry for sin (contrite and repentant).

Isaiah 66:2 *"For all these things My hand has made, So all these things came into being [by and for Me]," declares the Lord. "But to this one I will look [graciously], To him who is humble and contrite in spirit, and who [reverently] trembles at My word and honors My commands.*

2 Corinthians 7:10 ^{For} *[godly] sorrow that is in accord with the will of God produces a repentance without regret, leading to salvation; but worldly sorrow [the hopeless sorrow of those who do not believe] produces death.*

Luke 18:13-14 *But the tax collector, standing at a distance, would not even raise his eyes toward heaven, but was striking his chest [in humility and repentance], saying, 'God, be merciful and gracious to me, the [especially wicked] sinner [that I am]!'* ¹⁴ *I tell you, this man went to his home justified [forgiven of the guilt of sin and placed in right standing with God] rather than the other man; for everyone who exalts himself will be humbled, but he who humbles himself [forsaking self-righteous pride] will be exalted."*

What "h" word comes *before* being sorry for your sins? _____

What "r" word comes *after* being sorry for your sins? _____

This leads to what "s" word? _____

Why are all of these important? _____

Week 4 Day 6 Devotions: Re-read Psalm 4:7 and the following verses on joy.

Proverbs 17:22 *A happy heart is good medicine and a joyful mind causes healing, but a broken spirit dries up the bones.*

Proverbs 10:28 *The hope of the righteous [those of honorable character and integrity] is joy, But the expectation of the wicked [those who oppose God and ignore His wisdom] comes to nothing.*

Acts 13:52 *And the disciples were continually filled [throughout their hearts and souls] with joy and with the Holy Spirit.*

According to Proverbs 10 and Acts 13, what two things cause joy?

_____

_____

_____

What is the result of joy according to Proverbs 17?

_____

_____

_____

Name something that can bring you joy today.

_____

_____

_____

Week 4 Day 6 Devotions: Re-read Psalm 4:8 and the following verses on peace.

John 14:27 *Peace I leave with you; My [perfect] peace I give to you; not as the world gives do I give to you. Do not let your heart be troubled, nor let it be afraid. [Let My perfect peace calm you in every circumstance and give you courage and strength for every challenge.]*

Isaiah 26:3 *"You will keep in perfect and constant peace the one whose mind is steadfast [that is, committed and focused on You—in both inclination and character], Because he trusts and takes refuge in You [with hope and confident expectation].*

Philippians 4:6-7 *Do not be anxious or worried about anything, but in everything [every circumstance and situation] by prayer and petition with thanksgiving, continue to make your [specific] requests known to God. [7] And the peace of God [that peace which reassures the heart, that peace] which transcends all understanding, [that peace which] stands guard over your hearts and your minds in Christ Jesus [is yours].*

What kind of peace does God give you according to these three verses?

_____

_____

What must you do to receive peace according to Is. 26 and Phil. 4?

_____

_____

_____

What area of your life where you need God's peace right now? Write it down and give it to God.

_____

_____

_____

_____

Week 5 Day 1: Psalm 5

[1] *Listen to my words, O Lord, give heed to my sighing and groaning.*
[2] *Hear the sound of my cry, my King and my God, for to You do I pray.*
[3] *In the morning You hear my voice, O Lord; in the morning I prepare [a prayer, a sacrifice] for You and watch and wait [for You to speak to my heart].*
[4] *For You are not a God Who takes pleasure in wickedness; neither will the evil [man] so much as dwell [temporarily] with You.*
[5] *Boasters can have no standing in Your sight; You abhor all evildoers.*
[6] *You will destroy those who speak lies; the Lord abhors [and rejects] the bloodthirsty and deceitful man.*
[7] *But as for me, I will enter Your house through the abundance of Your steadfast love and mercy; I will worship toward and at Your holy temple in reverent fear and awe of You.*
[8] *Lead me, O Lord, in Your righteousness because of my enemies; make Your way level (straight and right) before my face.*
[9] *For there is nothing trustworthy or steadfast or truthful in their talk; their heart is destruction [or a destructive chasm, a yawning*

David is sighing and groaning as he prays to God in verse 1. He is not just calling out to God as he did in Psalm 4. He's crying out from the depths of his heart (vs.2). There is a sense of desperation here, which we will see several times as we read through the book of Psalms. David appears to be feeling low even as the day begins (vs. 3). A simple but important lesson can be learned from his actions. He sought God first thing. He didn't wallow in self-pity, call his friends over to pour out his problems to them, or bottle his feelings inside. His first response to his downcast emotions was to pray and to trust that God would hear his voice (vs. 3).

Before you get out of bed make a point to talk to God. Thank Him, list your concerns about the day, pray for others, and then watch and wait for Him to speak to your heart (vs. 3). Following these steps before you get busy, worried, or tired will change your life. It took a crisis to get me to make prayer and Bible study a priority in my life. Yes, I prayed often and throughout the day before the storm, but during it I became acutely aware of my need for God's strength and help. My eyes were open to the fact that many of my prayers had been somewhat shallow and sometimes haphazard. Now, I began to be conscious of what I said, how I said it, and how often I said it. Prayer was my lifeline and my battlefield. I hooked myself up to God like an IV fluid bag through prayer.

Sometimes I would simply whisper, "I trust you, God," "I need you, Jesus," "Thank you, Father," "I love you, Lord." Even these simple yet heartfelt prayers drew me closer to my shepherd. As I grew stronger through God's divine help, I added another component to my prayer time– I prayed for others. Again, I prayed for people all the time before the crisis, but my prayers changed. They were deeper, more genuine, more specific, and more powerful as God taught me to stand on His Word and trust in Him completely. Finally, because I was so desperately needed God during the struggle, I learned to listen. Too often we talk and ask but we don't listen. God gave us the Holy Spirit to be His voice to us (John 16:12-15). We need to make sure we

gulf]; their throat is an open sepulcher; they flatter and make smooth with their tongue.

¹⁰ Hold them guilty, O God; let them fall by their own designs and counsels; cast them out because of the multitude of their transgressions, for they have rebelled against You.

¹¹ But let all those who take refuge and put their trust in You rejoice; let them ever sing and shout for joy, because You make a covering over them and defend them; let those also who love Your name be joyful in You and be in high spirits.

¹² For You, Lord, will bless the [uncompromisingly] righteous [him who is upright and in right standing with You]; as with a shield You will surround him with goodwill (pleasure and favor).

Side Note:

Even if the world is dark and things are falling apart, speak truths like verse 11 and 12 over your life. God is often waiting for your words of faith and working behind the scenes while you are standing in faith (Daniel 10:12). Do it even when you don't feel like it. Do it even if your mind doesn't quite believe it yet. Eventually your mind will catch up with what you know

shut up long enough to give Him a chance to speak to our hearts. It is an overwhelming and beautiful thing to know you have heard God. It is an honor and a privilege not to be taken lightly.

Let us move on to verses 4-6 and 9. Here David tells us the source of his groaning. He is dealing with wicked people who boast, lie, and are out to bring others down. He reminds himself that these people do not dwell with God, they will be rejected, and eventually they will be destroyed. Sometimes we see so much evil in the world or see evil people prospering that we forget they are ultimately in God's hands. He will take care of them, so we can go ahead and give them to God. David also reminds himself that he dwells with God and is a recipient of God's abundant and never changing love and mercy (vs. 7). Is important to remember that God is love (1 John 4:16), He is merciful (Deuteronomy 4:31), and He never changes (Malachi 3:6). When we understand God's character and truly believe what His Word says about Him then we can trust Him completely, even when storms come, or we don't understand His plans for us.

In verses 8 and 10 David relies on the fact that God is righteous, without sin or flaw, so he trusts God to lead him down the straight and correct path and to take care of his enemies for him. Because God is righteous, He is also just (2 Thessalonians 1:6). He cannot allow sin to continue forever without punishment. If these wicked people do not put their trust in God and change their ways, they will be judged guilty by God. If they do not repent for their rebellion, they will be cast away from God. What a tragic place to be! Anywhere apart from God is empty and pain filled. Let us pray earnestly for those who are away from God. Let us take refuge in God so that we will never experience the destitution that being cast away from Him brings.

Finally, I would like to share how verses 11 and 12 have impacted my life. Verse 11 is hanging on the wall in my bedroom. I personalized many verses and spoke them aloud throughout the stormy years. Did you know you can do

to be true in your spirit when your ears hear it over and over again. Trust me because I have experienced this personally. Also, praise God and thank Him even when you don't feel like it. It will change your emotions and move mountains (but that is a topic for another time).

that– personalize scripture? These personalized promises become declarations of God's Word over our life. When we confess with our mouth the truths from the Word of God, He will cause things to move in the supernatural (unseen) and the natural (seen) realm (Proverbs 18:20-21, Mark 11:22-23).

Hearing these declarations out loud helps connect our spirit with our body. There is something special that happens when we speak and hear His promises out loud. Remember that God's Word is His will, so when you speak His Word out loud you are speaking His will in your life. Just be careful to keep verses in context. Verses 11 and 12 personalized: **"Father, my family and I take refuge in you. We trust you and we rejoice! We sing and shout for joy because You defend us! You cover us with your mighty hand, and we are joyful! Thank you, Father. You are our shield. You surround us from every side with your favor and goodness. Hallelujah!"**

This becomes your prayer of faith for chapter 5.

I encourage you to get excited about what this confession means. Shout, "HALLELUJAH!" at the fact that our mighty God defends us and surrounds us with His protection and favor! That makes me excited! It makes me rejoice, and I hope it does the same for you too.

Week 5 Day 1 Notes for Psalm 5: Which verse stood out to you the most and why?

_____

_____

_____

_____

What important life lesson can you apply from this Psalm?

_____

_____

_____

Week 5 Day 2 Devotions: Re-read Psalm 5:3 and the following verses on waiting.

Isaiah 30:18-19 *God Is Gracious and Just Therefore the Lord waits [expectantly] and longs to be gracious to you, And therefore He waits on high to have compassion on you. For the Lord is a God of justice; blessed (happy, fortunate) are all those who long for Him [since He will never fail them].*

Titus 2:13 *awaiting and confidently expecting the [fulfillment of our] blessed hope and the glorious appearing of our great God and Savior, Christ Jesus,*

Micah 7:7 *But as for me, I will look expectantly for the Lord and with confidence in Him I will keep watch; I will wait [with confident expectation] for the God of my salvation. My God will hear me.*

How does God wait for you and how you are to wait for Him according to these three verses?

_____

_____

_____

Have you ever thought about the fact that God longs to be gracious and compassionate toward you?

How do these characteristics show what kind of father He is?

_____

_____

_____

_____

Week 5 Day 3 Devotions: Re-read Psalm 5:5 and the following verses on pride.

Galatians 6:4 *But each one must carefully scrutinize his own work [examining his actions, attitudes, and behavior], and then he can have the personal satisfaction and inner joy of doing something commendable without comparing himself to another.*

Romans 12:3, 16 *For by the grace [of God] given to me I say to every one of you not to think more highly of himself [and of his importance and ability] than he ought to think; but to think so as to have sound judgment, as God has apportioned to each a degree of faith [and a purpose designed for service]. Live in harmony with one another; do not be haughty [conceited, self-important, exclusive], but associate with humble people [those with a realistic self-view]. Do not overestimate yourself.*

Isaiah 2:12 *For the Lord of hosts will have a day of reckoning Against all who are proud and arrogant and against all who are lifted up, that they may be degraded.*

What is the difference between the pride talked about in Galatians 6 and Romans 12?

_____

_____

_____

What will happen as a result of pride according to Isaiah 2?

_____

_____

Week 5 Day 4 Devotions: Re-read Psalm 5:7 and the following verses on God's love.

John 3:16 *"For God so [greatly] loved and dearly prized the world, that He [even] gave His [One and] only begotten Son, so that whoever believes and trusts in Him [as Savior] shall not perish, but have eternal life.*

Romans 8:37-39 *Yet in all these things we are more than conquerors and gain an overwhelming victory through Him who loved us [so much that He died for us]. For I am convinced [and continue to be convinced—beyond any doubt] that neither death, nor life, nor angels, nor principalities, nor things present and threatening, nor things to come, nor powers, nor height, nor depth, nor any other created thing, will be able to separate us from the [unlimited] love of God, which is in Christ Jesus our Lord.*

1 John 4:7-8 *Beloved, let us [unselfishly] love and seek the best for one another, for love is from God; and everyone who loves [others] is born of God and knows God [through personal experience]. ⁸ The one who does not love has not become acquainted with God [does not and never did know Him], for God is love. [He is the originator of love, and it is an enduring attribute of His nature.]*

What did God give you to show His love for you? _____

What does this gift give you according to Romans 8? _____

What kind of love should you have according to 1 John 4?

_____

_____

_____

Week 5 Day 5 Devotions: Re-read Psalm 5:8 and the following verses on God's righteousness.

Deuteronomy 32:4 *"The Rock! His work is perfect, for all His ways are just; A God of faithfulness without iniquity (injustice), Just and upright is He.*

Job 37:23 *"The Almighty—we cannot find Him; He is exalted in power and He will not do violence to [nor disregard] justice and abundant righteousness.*

Revelation 15:3 *And they sang the song of Moses, the bond-servant of God, and the song of the Lamb, saying, "Great and wonderful and awe-inspiring are Your works [in judgment], O Lord God, the Almighty [the Omnipotent, the Ruler of all]; Righteous and true are Your ways, O King of the nations!*

Why is it significant that one of God's characteristics is righteousness?

_____

_____

_____

How is Job's declaration of God's righteousness comforting to you, knowing that he endured great sorrow and still trusted God?

_____

_____

_____

Week 5 Day 6 Devotions: Re-read Psalm 5:10 and the following verses on God's reaction to those who reject Him.

2 Chronicles 7:19-20 *"But if you [people] turn away and abandon My statutes and My commandments which I have set before you, and you go and serve other gods and worship them, then I will uproot Israel from My land which I have given them; and I will cast this house, which I have consecrated for My Name, out of My sight, and will make it a proverb and an object of scorn among all nations.*

1 Samuel 15:23 *"For rebellion is as [serious as] the sin of divination (fortune-telling), Because you have rejected the word of the Lord, He also has rejected you as king."*

Deuteronomy 32:20 *"Then He said, 'I will hide My face from them, I will see what their end shall be; For they are a perverse generation, Sons in whom there is no faithfulness.*

Who do you know that has rejected God?

_____

_____

_____

_____

According to these verses, what will happen to them if they do not turn to Him

_____

_____

Pray for them right now.

Week 5 Day 7 Devotions: Re-read Psalm 5:11 and the following verses on God as our covering and defense.

Psalm 91:4 *He will cover you and completely protect you with His pinions, and under His wings you will find refuge; His faithfulness is a shield and a wall.*

2 Thessalonians 3:3 *But the Lord is faithful, and He will strengthen you [setting you on a firm foundation] and will protect and guard you from the evil one.*

Psalm 94:22 *But the Lord has become my high tower and defense, and my God the rock of my refuge.*

Because God is _____ He protects you, _____ you, and guards you.

How does relying on His faithfulness, rather than your own, make you feel?

_____

_____

What can you do to put yourself under His wings today?

_____

_____

_____

_____

Week 6 Day 1: Psalm 6

¹ O Lord, rebuke me not in Your anger nor discipline and chasten me in Your hot displeasure.
² Have mercy on me and be gracious to me, O Lord, for I am weak (faint and withered away); O Lord, heal me, for my bones are troubled.
³ My [inner] self [as well as my body] is also exceedingly disturbed and troubled. But You, O Lord, how long [until You return and speak peace to me]?
⁴ Return [to my relief], O Lord, deliver my life; save me for the sake of Your steadfast love and mercy.
⁵ For in death there is no remembrance of You; in Sheol (the place of the dead) who will give You thanks?
⁶ I am weary with my groaning; all night I soak my pillow with tears, I drench my couch with my weeping.
⁷ My eye grows dim because of grief; it grows old because of all my enemies.
⁸ Depart from me, all you workers of iniquity, for the Lord has heard the voice of my weeping.
⁹ The Lord has heard my supplication; the Lord receives my prayer.
¹⁰ Let all my enemies be ashamed and sorely troubled; let them turn back and be put to shame suddenly.

Psalm 6 is one of several Psalms where David has sinned in some way, and he is remorseful and repentant over his actions. It is believed that this may be a Psalm he wrote after he sinned with Bathsheba. In verses 1 and 2 David realizes that his sin has angered God. He knows that God is righteous and just and, therefore, must punish sin. He knows he is deserving of punishment but is pleading with God to be merciful. His grief over his sin and ensuing consequences has made him physically and mentally sick.

Have you ever been anxious because you didn't know what was going to happen next? I'm not talking about the excited version of anxious, like when you were a child waiting to tear into your Christmas presents or riding your first ride at Disney World. I am talking about the nervous version, like when you're waiting for a root canal or when you have gotten news that someone you love was in a terrible accident and the doctor doesn't know if they will make it. I believe that David may be feeling like this in verse 3 when he says that his inner self and his body are greatly disturbed and troubled. He goes on to ask God where He is and when He will return. David has lost his peace and he needs desperately for God to wash over him with divine peace.

Anxiety feels like someone is blending your insides in a food processor. Your heart flutters uncontrollably at the minimum and pounds so much it literally hurts at its worst. Physically, even with proper breathing, soothing music, and other forms of relaxation, anxiety at its worst cannot be controlled and is barely bearable at its minimum. Anxiety is different from depression in that it is a heightening of a person's senses and emotions, while depression suppresses and lowers functions.

David didn't just physically feel troubled; his mind was troubled too (vs.3). An anxious person's thoughts race, and the same dreadful or unsure thoughts will replay over and over like a stutter. Even chemical processes in the brain change, which is why so many people turn to medicine to soothe anxiety's symptoms (see side note). David feels such unease that he feels like God has left him (vs. 3). He is in

Side Note: adaa.org and dbsalliance.org

1. Anxiety disorders affect 40 million adults in the United States. The average age of onset is 11 years old.
2. Anxiety disorders are highly treatable, yet only about 1/3 of those suffering receive treatment.
3. Anxiety disorders and depression disorders develop from a complex set of risk factors, including genetics, brain chemistry, personality, and life events.
4. Depression affects approximately 14.8 million American adults and is the is the cause of over 2/3 of the 30,000 reported suicides in the U.S. each year.
5. For every 2 homicides committed in the United States, there are 3 suicides.
6. Untreated depression is the number 1 risk for suicide among youth. Suicide is the 3rd leading cause of death in 15 to 24 year-olds and the 4th leading cause of death in 10 to 14 year-olds. Young males aged 15 to 24 are at highest risk for suicide.
7. Despite its high treatment success rate, nearly 2 out of 3 people suffering with depression do not actively seek nor receive proper treatment.

such distress that he can't see God or feel his presence (vs. 4). He pleads for God to save him. He even feels as if he might die because of the stress (vs. 5).

Now, David did have many enemies who wanted to harm him; so, he very well may have had a real reason to fear for his life in verse 5, but in this Psalm he seems to be talking about dying from grief. We must realize that David is depressed, as well as anxious, which can cause an overreaction to situations. He tells us in verses 6 & 7 that he has cried so much it has made him weary. His eyes hurt and are blurry because of the tears. He feels overwhelmed and old, and his heart grieves. David literally feels pain because of the emotional turmoil he is experiencing due to his sin and his enemies.

Human emotions are very powerful and can stem from truth or misperceptions. Either way, depression and anxiety start from a seed and are watered by thoughts, outside forces, and chemical imbalances. They can also be caused by a spiritual attack. Depression, as well as other emotions, can skew a person's point of view so that their eyes, ears, and thoughts process situations inappropriately or incorrectly. This only makes the depression or anxiety worse, and it needs to be dealt with by a Christian psychologist or medical professional as soon as possible (see side note).

As for David, his first response is to pray in vs. 4 and his prayer is answered in between vs. 7 & 8. All of a sudden strength rises up in David's Spirit. His mind clears. His eyes see. His wave of emotion subsides. What we see next is an absolute 180^0 from the earlier verses. He has a revelation from God, as if God has spoken to him directly and said, "David, it's done! Buck up, dust yourself off and have courage because I have it all under control!" David declares that his enemies shall depart from him at this instant because God has heard his cries and taken pity on his tears (vs. 8, 9).

He knows in his heart that he is forgiven of his sin and that he has victory through God over his enemies. They are the ones who will be troubled. They're the ones who will feel shame. They will now experience the curse of anxiety and depression because of what they have done to God's chosen king (vs. 10).

Prayer: God, I know my mind and emotions can sometimes get the best of me. Deliver me from any negative emotion that would grab hold of me, cloud my judgment, or change my perceptions. Cause me to see clearly through the power of the Holy Spirit. Wash over me with your divine peace because of your great love and mercy. I turn my eyes and thoughts to you Lord. In Jesus name I pray, Amen.

We too should know in our hearts that God hears us, forgives us, and can heal our emotions. Turn to Him first and talk to your pastor or a spiritual leader in your church, but do not feel shame in getting further assistance if the problem persists or interferes with your everyday activities. If you do not have a problem with anxiety or depression, then please watch out for other people whom you think may be experiencing these emotions. Pray for them and with them and encourage them to receive treatment if necessary. Be patient and understanding. Too often people don't know what to do and couldn't do it anyway because their mind and judgment are clouded by strong emotions and uncontrollable chemical reactions. God can do a mighty work in you or them just like he did for David in this Psalm, but He can also work through you, a pastor, psychologist, or doctor.

Week 6 Day 1 Notes for Psalm 6: Which verse stood out to you the most and why?

_____

_____

_____

_____

What important life lesson can you apply from this Psalm?

_____

_____

_____

_____

Week 6 Day 2 Devotions: Re-read Psalm 6:1 and the following verses on God's discipline.

Hebrews 12:6 *For the Lord disciplines and corrects those whom He loves, And He punishes every son whom He receives and welcomes [to His heart]."*

Revelation 3:19 *Those whom I [dearly and tenderly] love, I rebuke and discipline [showing them their faults and instructing them]; so be enthusiastic and repent [change your inner self—your old way of thinking, your sinful behavior—seek God's will].*

Job 5:17 *"Behold, how happy and fortunate is the man whom God reproves, So do not despise or reject the discipline of the Almighty [subjecting you to trial and suffering].*

Who does God discipline? _____

What does His discipline bring about in you according to Revelations 3?

_____

_____

_____

How should you react to the discipline?

_____

_____

_____

Week 6 Day 3 Devotions: Re-read Psalm 6:2-3 and the following verses on a troubled heart/anxiety.

John 14:1 *"Do not let your heart be troubled (afraid, cowardly). Believe [confidently] in God and trust in Him, [have faith, hold on to it, rely on it, keep going and] believe also in Me.*

Luke 12:25 *And which of you by worrying can add one hour to his life's span?*

Peter 5:7 *casting all your cares [all your anxieties, all your worries, and all your concerns, once and for all] on Him, for He cares about you [with deepest affection, and watches over you very carefully].*

Is there something you are anxious about today?

_____

_____

_____

What are you supposed to do when you feel anxious, according to John 14 and Peter 5?

_____

_____

_____

_____

Week 6 Day 4 Devotions: Re-read Psalm 6:4 and the following verses on God's deliverance.

Psalm 34:17 *When the righteous cry [for help], the Lord hears and rescues them from all their distress and troubles.*

Psalm 107:6 *Then they cried out to the Lord in their trouble, And He rescued them from their distresses.*

2 Samuel 22:2 *He said: "The Lord is my rock and my fortress [on the mountain] and my rescuer (deliverer);*

When you are in distress what will God do for you?

_____

List 2 or 3 people you know who are in distress and need this good news today?

_____

_____

Pray for them now and ask God to give you an opportunity to share the Word with them.

Week 6 Day 5 Devotions: Read the following verses on repentance.

Acts 3:19 *So repent [change your inner self—your old way of thinking, regret past sins] and return [to God—seek His purpose for your life], so that your sins may be wiped away [blotted out, completely erased], so that times of refreshing may come from the presence of the Lord [restoring you like a cool wind on a hot day];*

2 Chronicles 7:14 *and My people, who are called by My Name, humble themselves, and pray and seek (crave, require as a necessity) My face and turn from their wicked ways, then I will hear [them] from heaven, and forgive their sin and heal their land.*

Proverbs 28:13 *He who conceals his transgressions will not prosper, but whoever confesses and turns away from his sins will find compassion and mercy.*

According to Acts 3, what does repent mean?

_____

_____

List the promises God will do for you when you repent, according to these 3 verses?

_____

_____

_____

Go ahead and confess your sins today and receive His repentance.

Week 6 Day 6 Devotions: Re-read Psalm 6:6-7 and the following verses on weariness and upheaval in your spirit.

Matthew 11:28-29 (AMPC) *Come to Me, all you who labor and are heavy-laden and overburdened, and I will cause you to rest. [I will ease and relieve and refresh your souls. Take My yoke upon you and learn of Me, for I am gentle (meek) and humble (lowly) in heart, and you will find rest (relief and ease and refreshment and recreation and blessed quiet) for your souls.*

Psalm 42:11 *Why are you in despair, O my soul? Why have you become restless and disquieted within me? Hope in God and wait expectantly for Him, for I shall yet praise Him, The help of my countenance and my God.*

2 Corinthians 1:3-4 *Blessed [gratefully praised and adored] be the God and Father of our Lord Jesus Christ, the Father of mercies and the God of all comfort, who comforts and encourages us in every trouble so that we will be able to comfort and encourage those who are in any kind of trouble, with the comfort with which we ourselves are comforted by God.*

Briefly describe a time when you have experienced weariness or upheaval in your spirit.

_____

_____

_____

What 3 things does God tell you to do in Matthew 11?

_____

_____

What does He promise to do for you?

_____

_____

After He does His part and comforts you, what are you supposed to do according to 2 Corinthians?

_____

_____

_____

_____

Week 6 Day 7 Devotions: Re-read Psalm 6:8-9 and the following verses on God hearing us.

1 John 5:*14* *This is the [remarkable degree of] confidence which we [as believers are entitled to] have before Him: that if we ask anything according to His will, [that is, consistent with His plan and purpose] He hears us.*

Jeremiah 29:11-12 *For I know the plans and thoughts that I have for you,' says the Lord, 'plans for peace and well-being and not for disaster to give you a future and a hope. Then you will call on Me and you will come and pray to Me, and I will hear [your voice] and I will listen to you.*

Proverbs 15:29 *The Lord is far from the wicked [and distances Himself from them], But He hears the prayer of the [consistently] righteous [that is, those with spiritual integrity and moral courage].*

What are the prerequisites (actions required of you) in these verses for you to be confident that God hears your prayers?

_____

_____

_____

_____

What does knowing that God hears your prayers mean to you?

_____

_____

_____

_____

Week 7 Day 1: Psalm 7

¹ O Lord my God, in You I take refuge and put my trust; save me from all those who pursue and persecute me, and deliver me,
² Lest my foe tear my life [from my body] like a lion, dragging me away while there is none to deliver.
³ O Lord my God, if I have done this, if there is wrong in my hands,
⁴ If I have paid back with evil him who was at peace with me or without cause have robbed him who was my enemy,
⁵ Let the enemy pursue my life and take it; yes, let him trample my life to the ground and lay my honor in the dust. Selah [pause, and calmly think of that]!
⁶ Arise, O Lord, in Your anger; lift up Yourself against the rage of my enemies; and awake [and stir up] for me the justice and vindication [that] You have commanded.
⁷ Let the assembly of the peoples be gathered about You, and return on high over them.
⁸ The Lord judges the people; judge me, O Lord, and do me justice according to my righteousness [my rightness, justice, and right standing with You] and according to the integrity that is in me.

⁹ Oh, let the wickedness of the wicked come to an end, but establish the [uncompromisingly]

Saul became threatened by praise David was receiving from the people for slaying Goliath. He chased him and wanted to kill him. Instead of being honored for his bravery, David found himself on the run and hiding in a cave. This is the setting for Psalm 7.

In times of trouble, we need to take refuge in our heavenly Father (vs. 1). Notice what often comes from our mouths in times when we can't change our circumstances or fix the problem: "Well, all we can do now is pray." Too often, after we have exhausted our resources, we turn to God for help. Prayer should not be our last resort. Trusting in and relying on God should not be an afterthought when there's nothing left to be done in the natural realm. We should turn to Him first, then take action as He leads us and continue to trust Him through the trial (see side note).

David has people wanting to tear him up like a lion eating its prey (vs. 2). Who better to turn to than God? Verses 3-5 show us that David is confident that God will rescue him. He is confident that he is innocently being persecuted. He basically tells God, "Look, if I have sinned against anyone, then let them catch me and trample me to the ground!" He goes on to call upon God's just nature and reminds God of his past promises in order to receive divine vindication.

I would like to briefly explain what vindication is and give you some scriptures to research this topic more. It is important to understand that there is justice for our righteousness- right living and right standing with God (vs. 8). As we live with integrity (live according to what we believe and profess) we can expect God's vindication. Vindication is being cleared, acquitted, defended, or exonerated from an accusation. We are first and foremost vindicated by the blood of the cross so that we will be found guiltless when we are judged at the end of time (1 Corinthians 1:8 and 2 Corinthians 5:10). However, we can also expect vindication on earth if we are wrongly judged (Isaiah 54:17, Luke 18:7-8).

This is what David is talking about in verses 6, 8, 10 and 11. God does not allow his people to live under persecution without justice in the end. Many times, justice and

righteous [those upright and in harmony with You]; for You, Who try the hearts and emotions and thinking powers, are a righteous God.
10 My shield and my defense depend on God, Who saves the upright in heart.
11 God is a righteous judge, And a God who is indignant every day.
12 If a man does not turn and repent, [God] will whet His sword; He has strung and bent His [huge] bow and made it ready [by treading it with His foot].
13 He has also prepared for him deadly weapons; He makes His arrows fiery shafts.
14 Behold, [the wicked man] conceives iniquity and is pregnant with mischief and gives birth to lies.
15 He made a pit and hollowed it out and has fallen into the hole which he made [before the trap was completed].
16 His mischief shall fall back in return upon his own head, and his violence come down [with the loose dirt] upon his own scalp.
17 I will give to the Lord the thanks due to His rightness and justice, and I will sing praise to the name of the Lord Most High.

Side Note: gallup.com

1. 74% of Americans said they prayed more than usual

vindication do not come in our timing, and they may not even come in the form we want or expect it to. Sometimes full justice and vindication come as we enter into the richness of Heaven after we depart from this earth. Our job while we wait is to make God our refuge, trust in Him, and honor His commands (vs. 6).

It can be very difficult to wait for God's justice, especially in the heat of turmoil, but it is what we must do in order to stand strong and pass to the other side of the situation. This idea is touched on in verse 9 when David says God will establish those in harmony with Him, who tries the heart, emotions, and thoughts. Try means to test until purified. Sometimes God will allow situations into our lives that will cause us to have to rely on Him. Sometimes we are tried, tested, so that we can be purified and brought closer to Him. Sometimes we are tested so we learn a valuable lesson that we will need in the future. These times are never fun and may even be painful but are necessary for our good and the good of those we will be able to minister to after having grown through these times.

Let me be clear about something. I do not believe that God causes evil to happen to people in order to accomplish His purposes in their lives (James 1:13, 1 John 1:5, 1 Corinthians 14:33 and 10:13). He is a good God, a just God, and free of evil, so he cannot by His nature cause evil. He did test, try, people's obedience and caused judgments to be brought on the Israelites and opposing nations in the Old Testament when they failed to obey. He will also cause judgment on wicked men (vs. 12). However, in all cases He has made his expectations and consequences very clear beforehand (we discussed this in Psalm 2).

He is not a master chess player orchestrating every single move in our lives, unless we give him permission and free reign to do so, because that would take away our free will. Because of free will, we choose our own path. Because of the choices we make, or the choices of others, we experience consequences (good or bad depending on the original cause). God allows our causes to have effects, and unfortunately

after the terrorist attacks of Sept. 11, 2001.

2. A March 2003 poll showed 52% of the population reported praying more because of the war with Iraq.

Prayer: Heavenly Father, I praise you and give you honor because you are the one true God. Give me strength as you try my heart. May I come out pure and not forget the lessons I have learned from the process. I give you full reign in my life. I rely on you as my defense and shield against anything or anyone who would come against me. I thank you for your justice and vindication. I love you Lord, Amen.

sometimes our lives are drastically and negatively changed by sinful choices we make or the wickedness of others. Be sure of one thing: if we are harmed by the sin of others, we will be vindicated, and they will be judged.

The wicked birth what is in their hearts, mischief and lies (vs. 14). They dig pits to trap others but eventually fall into the pits themselves (vs. 15). What they mean for evil against others will come back on them swiftly and violently (vs. 16). God can even use the evil that was meant to harm us and turn it into something good in our lives and in the lives of others (Genesis 50:20, Romans 8:28). This is why we give thanks to God, for His righteousness and justice (vs. 17). This is why we praise and honor the one true God.

Week 7 Day 1 Notes for Psalm 7: Which verse stood out to you the most and why?

_____

_____

_____

What important life lesson can you apply from this Psalm?

_____

_____

_____

Week 7 Day 2 Devotions: Re-read Psalm 7:1 and the following verses on God as your refuge.

Psalm 46:1-2 *God is our refuge and strength [mighty and impenetrable], A very present and well-proved help in trouble. Therefore we will not fear, though the earth should change and though the mountains be shaken and slip into the heart of the seas,*

2 Samuel 22:2-3 *He said: "The Lord is my rock and my fortress [on the mountain] and my rescuer; My God, my rock, in whom I take refuge; My shield and the horn of my salvation, my stronghold and my refuge, My Savior—You save me from violence.*

Psalm 61:3 *For You have been a shelter and a refuge for me, A strong tower against the enemy.*

What benefits do you have when you make God your refuge?

_____

_____

List a few people you know today who need a place of refuge because of circumstances in their life?

_____

_____

Pray for them now.

Week 7 Day 3 Devotions: Re-read Psalm 7:2 and the following verses on people/Satan hurting you.

1 Peter 5:8 *Be sober [well balanced and self-disciplined], be alert and cautious at all times. That enemy of yours, the devil, prowls around like a roaring lion [fiercely hungry], seeking someone to devour.*

Psalm 27:10 *Although my father and my mother have abandoned me, Yet the Lord will take me up [adopt me as His child].*

Romans 12:17 *Never repay anyone evil for evil. Take thought for what is right and gracious and proper in the sight of everyone.*

How do you keep from getting hurt by Satan according to 1 Peter 5?

_____

_____

Who will never hurt you or leave you?

_____

_____

According to Romans 12, what should your response be to being hurt?

_____

_____

Week 7 Day 4 Devotions: Re-read Psalm 7:6 and the following verses on God's anger.

John 3:36 *He who believes and trusts in the Son and accepts Him [as Savior] has eternal life [that is, already possesses it]; but he who does not believe the Son and chooses to reject Him, [disobeying Him and denying Him as Savior] will not see [eternal] life, but [instead] the wrath of God hangs over him continually."*

Ephesians 5:6 *Let no one deceive you with empty arguments [that encourage you to sin], for because of these things the wrath of God comes upon the sons of disobedience [those who habitually sin].*

Romans 1:18 *For [God does not overlook sin and] the wrath of God is revealed from heaven against all ungodliness and unrighteousness of men who in their wickedness suppress and stifle the truth,*

What makes God angry according to these verses?

_____

_____

_____

According to these verses, what can you do to avoid God's wrath?

_____

_____

_____

Week 7 Day 5 Devotions: Re-read Psalm 7:6 and the following verses on God's vindication.

Isaiah 54:17 *"No weapon that is formed against you will succeed; And every tongue that rises against you in judgment you will condemn. This [peace, righteousness, security, and triumph over opposition] is the heritage of the servants of the Lord, And this is their vindication from Me," says the Lord.*

Deuteronomy 32:35-36 NIV *It is mine to avenge; I will repay. In due time their foot will slip; their day of disaster is near and their doom rushes upon them." The Lord will vindicate his people and relent concerning his servants when he sees their strength is gone and no one is left, slave or free.*

1 Corinthians 1:8 AMPC *And He will establish you to the end [keep you steadfast, give you strength, and guarantee your vindication; He will be your warrant against all accusation or indictment so that you will be] guiltless and irreproachable in the day of our Lord Jesus Christ (the Messiah).*

What brings you peace and victory according to Is. 54?

_____

_____

What is the definition of vindication according to 1 Cor.?

_____

_____

_____

What does it mean to you that God will establish you?

_____

_____

_____

Week 7 Day 6 Devotions: Re-read Psalm 7:8 and the following verses on God's judgment.

Proverbs 21:2 *Every man's way is right in his own eyes, But the Lord weighs and examines the hearts [of people and their motives].*

Isaiah 13:11 *In this way I will punish the world for its evil And the wicked for their wickedness [their sin, their injustice, their wrongdoing]; I will also put an end to the arrogance of the proud And will abase the arrogance of the tyrant.*

2 Corinthians 5:10 *For we [believers will be called to account and] must all appear before the judgment seat of Christ, so that each one may be repaid for what has been done in the body, whether good or bad [that is, each will be held responsible for his actions, purposes, goals, motives—the use or misuse of his time, opportunities and abilities].*

Write about anything in your past or your heart today that could bring God's judgment because you have not given it to Him or repented? Won't you stop right now and put it under the blood of Jesus?

_____

_____

_____

_____

Week 7 Day 7 Devotions: Re-read Psalm 7:15-16 and the following verses on sewing and reaping.

Job 18:8 *"For the wicked is thrown into a net by his own feet (wickedness), and he steps on the webbing [of the lattice-covered pit].*

Proverbs 22:8 *He who sows injustice will reap [a harvest of] trouble, and the rod of his wrath [with which he oppresses others] will fail.*

Galatians 6:7-8 *Do not be deceived, God is not mocked [He will not allow Himself to be ridiculed, nor treated with contempt nor allow His precepts to be scornfully set aside]; for whatever a man sows, this and this only is what he will reap. ⁸ For the one who sows to his flesh [his sinful capacity, his worldliness, his disgraceful impulses] will reap from the flesh ruin and destruction, but the one who sows to the Spirit will from the Spirit reap eternal life.*

Put the principle of sowing and reaping, as described in these verses, in your own words.

_____

_____

_____

_____

What are you sowing that is bad in your life?

_____

_____

_____

_____

What are you sowing that is good in your life?

_____

_____

_____

_____

Week 8 Day 1: Psalm 8

¹ O Lord, our Lord, how excellent (majestic and glorious) is Your name in all the earth! You have set Your glory on [or above] the heavens.
² Out of the mouths of babes and unweaned infants You have established strength because of Your foes, that You might silence the enemy and the avenger.
³ When I view and consider Your heavens, the work of Your fingers, the moon and the stars, which You have ordained and established,
⁴ What is man that You are mindful of him, and the son of [earthborn] man that You care for him?
⁵ Yet You have made him but a little lower than God [or heavenly beings], and You have crowned him with glory and honor.
⁶ You made him to have dominion over the works of Your hands; You have put all things under his feet:
⁷ All sheep and oxen, yes, and the beasts of the field,
⁸ The birds of the air, and the fish of the sea, and whatever passes along the paths of the seas.
⁹ O Lord, our Lord, how excellent (majestic and glorious) is Your name in all the earth!

Is it any wonder that so many worship songs and hymns are rooted in the Psalms? Psalm chapter 8 is a great example of David's heart toward God and how our hearts should be as well. He is not asking for anything. He's not anxious, depressed, or fearful. He is simply but deeply pouring his heart out to his heavenly Father. He stands in awe of God's greatness. He praises God for *who* He is and worships Him with purity, not for *what* He has personally done for him.

It is vital for believers to take time each day to worship God in sincerity for *who* He is. He is excellent and does everything with excellence. He is majestic and glorious beyond our comprehension. He is higher than anyone or anything in the entire universe (vs. 1). How can we not put him in that rightful place in our own daily lives?

David tells us in verse 2 that even infants and young children without experience and knowledge realize who God is and sing his praises with pureness of heart (Matthew 21:15, 16). Because of this genuine worship, there is strength over the enemy (vs. 2). God will silence the enemy and avenger for you because of your praise! Can I get an amen!

If you or a loved one is facing any kind of attack in your life right now it, is because of your enemy Satan. He hates you and is the cause of all evil that comes against you. Stop right now, reread verse 2, and praise God out loud (if you are in a public place, you can do this in your heart, but try not to get distracted). You aren't thanking Him for what you have or what He has done; you are worshiping Him for *who* He is. Do this especially if you don't feel like it– please trust me. If you can't think of anything specific to say read verse 1 out loud over and over again, meditating on it. You can also start with a worship song or say something simple like this: "I worship you father. I praise you with my whole heart. You are holy and worthy of my praise. You are glorious and awesome…" I hope you paused for a few moments to participate in the activity and feel refreshed and closer to God for it. God uses moments like that to silence Satan and quiet your spirit. He turns our worship into victory!

¹⁰ My defense and shield depend on God, Who saves the upright in heart.
¹¹ God is a righteous Judge, yes, a God Who is indignant every day.

Side Note: space.com

1. Due to the Hubble telescope launched in 1990, astronomers believe there are over 100 billion galaxies in our universe.
2. There are over 100 billion stars just in the Milky Way galaxy.

Prayer: Before praying, reread the concepts in the last paragraph slowly and meditate on them. It is vital that you understand who you are to God and what He has done for you.

I worship you, Lord. I want the way I live my life to honor you. You are worthy of honor, glory, and praise. You are the masterful Creator, and you care for me deeply. Thank you for silencing Satan's lies and his attack on me, my loved ones, and friends. You have placed your spirit and your glory in me. You have put everything under my feet. I am a good steward of your wondrous creation and victorious over Satan through your power in me. Thank you! Amen

David moves on in verse 3 to express God's magnificence and power by recounting the creation of the moon and stars. I can picture David sitting on a hillside overseeing the harvest as the last bit of sunlight fades beyond the horizon. The farmers have cleaned their tools and tended to the animals before disappearing into their homes. A cool breeze brushes across his face as he surveys the land and leans back on his pack to look up at the sky. The stars are bright, and the moon is full. He starts to relax his mind and lets God come and rest on him. Inspiration and awe wash over him as he is overwhelmed by God's presence, holiness, and greatness. He picks up his loot and begins to play a tune, stops to sing his worship song, and continues to play as the worship song completely unfolds. Can you see it? Can you hear his song as you read Psalms 8? Can you hear God's voice speaking to David inspiring him? God can speak to you too if you will make time for Him, stop, and listen.

God's voice placed every star in its place, but His mighty hands gently formed man (see side note). In light of God's awesomeness and the vastness of the universe, we are so small and seemingly insignificant. Yet verse 4 says that we are cared for by the Creator himself, and verse 5 says that He breathed His life and spirit into us and made us "but a little lower than" Himself. He crowned us with glory and honor (favor and excellence). Because we have His very breath, spirit, in us we have His glory, His divine nature, in us (2 Corinthians 3:17-18). He has honored us (privileged us with favor) by allowing us to partake so intimately of Him. He is jealous, vigorously protective of the integrity of our relationship, and keeps us as the apple of His eye (Exodus 34:14, Psalm 17:8, and Zechariah 2:8). He has given us honor (given us special rank and distinction) by placing us in charge over His precious creation (vs. 6). All things are under our feet including our enemy (Romans 16:20).

Week 8 Day 1 Notes for Psalm 8: Which verse stood out to you the most and why?

_____

_____

_____

_____

What important life lesson can you apply from this Psalm?

_____

_____

_____

_____

Week 8 Day 2 Devotions: Re-read Psalm 8: 1 and the following verses about God's glory.

Exodus 33:9-10 *Whenever Moses entered the tent, the pillar of cloud would descend and stand at the doorway of the tent; and the Lord would speak with Moses. When all the people saw the pillar of cloud standing at the tent door, all the people would rise and worship, each at his tent door.*

Deuteronomy 5:24 *and you said, 'Behold, the Lord our God has shown us His glory and His greatness, and we have heard His voice from the midst of the fire; we have seen today that God speaks with man, yet he [still] lives.*

John 1:14 *And the Word (Christ) became flesh, and lived among us; and we [actually] saw His glory, glory as belongs to the [One and] only begotten Son of the Father, [the Son who is truly unique, the only One of His kind, who is] full of grace and truth (absolutely free of deception).*

Which 2 of the 5 senses is talked about in these 3 verses? _____

Why are they significant? _____

What does the fact that God, in all His magnificent glory, speaks to us and sent His son as a manifestation of His glory show you?

_____

_____

_____

_____

Week 8 Day 3 Devotions: Re-read Psalm 8: 2 and the following verses about how God silences the enemy.

Proverbs 16:7 *When a man's ways please the Lord, He makes even his enemies to be at peace with him.*

Daniel 6:22 *My God has sent His angel and has shut the mouths of the lions so that they have not hurt me, because I was found innocent before Him; and also before you, O king, I have committed no crime."*

Psalm 63:11 *But the king will rejoice in God; Everyone who swears by Him [honoring the true God, acknowledging His authority and majesty] will glory, For the mouths of those who speak lies will be stopped.*

According to Proverbs and Daniel, why will God help you in the face of enemies?

_____

_____

What physical and spiritual enemies are you facing right now?

_____

_____

_____

Honor God and watch what He will do for you.

Week 8 Day 4 Devotions: Re-read Psalm 8:3 and the following verses on God's creation.

Colossians 1:16-17 *For by Him all things were created in heaven and on earth, [things] visible and invisible, whether thrones or dominions or rulers or authorities; all things were created and exist through Him [that is, by His activity] and for Him. And He Himself existed and is before all things, and in Him all things hold together. [His is the controlling, cohesive force of the universe.]*

Isaiah 40:26 *Lift up your eyes on high and see who has created these heavenly bodies, The One who brings out their host by number, He calls them all by name; Because of the greatness of His might and the strength of His power, not one is missing.*

Jeremiah 32:17 *'Ah Lord God! Behold, You have made the heavens and the earth by Your great power and by Your outstretched arm! There is nothing too difficult or too wonderful for You—*

In a few words write down the most important ideas you learn from these verses about God as our creator.

_____

_____

_____

Week 8 Day 5 Devotions: Re-read Psalm 8:4 and the following verses about how God created man.

Genesis 1:27 *So God created man in His own image, in the image and likeness of God He created him; male and female He created them.*

Psalm 139:13-14 *For You formed my innermost parts; You knit me [together] in my mother's womb. I will give thanks and praise to You, for I am fearfully and wonderfully made; Wonderful are Your works, And my soul knows it very well.*

Jeremiah 1:5 *"Before I formed you in the womb I knew you [and approved of you as My chosen instrument], and before you were born I consecrated you [to Myself as My own]; I have appointed you as a prophet to the nations."*

God's works are wonderful and you are one of them. You have been created for a purpose. List 3 of your best qualities.

_____

_____

How can these characteristics help you fulfill your purpose?

_____

_____

Week 8 Day 6 Devotions: Re-read Psalm 8:4-6 and the following verses on our God given authority.

Genesis 1:26 *Then God said, "Let Us (Father, Son, Holy Spirit) make man in Our image, according to Our likeness [not physical, but a spiritual personality and moral likeness]; and let them have complete authority over the fish of the sea, the birds of the air, the cattle, and over the entire earth, and over everything that creeps and crawls on the earth."*

Luke 10:19 *Listen carefully: I have given you authority [that you now possess] to tread on [a]serpents and scorpions, and [the ability to exercise authority] over all the power of the enemy (Satan); and nothing will [in any way] harm you.*

Matthew 18:18-20 *I assure you and most solemnly say to you, whatever you bind [forbid, declare to be improper and unlawful] on earth shall have [already] been bound in heaven, and whatever you loose [permit, declare lawful] on earth shall have [already] been loosed in heaven.*

What do you have authority over according to these verses?

_____

_____

According to Matthew, how can you use your God given authority?

_____

_____

_____

Week 8 Day 7 Devotions: Re-read Psalm 8:11 and the following verses about God's majesty.

Job 37:22 *"Out of the north comes golden splendor [and people can hardly look on it]; Around God is awesome splendor and majesty [far too glorious for man's eyes].*

Exodus 15:11 *"Who is like You among the gods, O Lord? Who is like You, majestic in holiness, Awesome in splendor, working wonders?*

1 Chronicles 29:11 *Yours, O Lord, is the greatness and the power and the glory and the victory and the majesty, indeed everything that is in the heavens and on the earth; Yours is the dominion and kingdom, O Lord, and You exalt Yourself as head over all.*

Majesty is defined as supreme greatness or authority, sovereignty. How is God's majesty physically described in Job 37?

_____

_____

What does God's sovereignty give Him according to 1 Chronicles?

_____

_____

How can you give God complete authority in your life today?

_____

_____

_____

Week 9 Day 1: Psalm 9

¹ I will praise You, O Lord, with my whole heart; I will show forth (recount and tell aloud) all Your marvelous works and wonderful deeds!
² I will rejoice in You and be in high spirits; I will sing praise to Your name, O Most High!
³ When my enemies turned back, they stumbled and perished before You.
⁴ For You have maintained my right and my cause; You sat on the throne judging righteously.
⁵ You have rebuked the nations, You have destroyed the wicked; You have blotted out their name forever and ever.
⁶ The enemy have been cut off and have vanished in everlasting ruins, You have plucked up and overthrown their cities; the very memory of them has perished and vanished.
⁷ But the Lord shall remain and continue forever; He has prepared and established His throne for judgment.
⁸ And He will judge the world in righteousness (rightness and equity); He will minister justice to the peoples in uprightness.
⁹ The Lord also will be a refuge and a high tower for the oppressed, a refuge and a stronghold in times of trouble (high cost, destitution, and desperation).

We move from worshiping God for who He is in Psalm 8 to praising God for all His marvelous works and wonderful deeds in Psalm 9. In our prayer time, we should start with "Hallowed be Thy name" like Jesus did in Matthew 6:9. This is what we discussed in Psalm 8 when we worship God in reverence and genuineness for *who* He is. After this, I encourage you to praise Him and thank Him for what He has done, is currently doing, and even for what you believe He will do in your life. This is the "Give us this day our daily bread and forgive us our debts" part of the Lord's Prayer. David follows this pattern of prayer often in the Psalms and makes his requests afterward.

As we make praising God and thanking Him part of our daily prayers, we also need to remember to tell others what God has done for us (vs. 1). Our answered prayer, favor, and blessings are part of our testimony. As we rejoice in the Lord and are in high spirits, we are showing others how awesome He is (vs. 2). Our faces, attitudes, and words are to be a reflection of His goodness.

What God did for David, He will do for you as well. God turned David's enemies away from him and held David up in his hands (vs. 3-7). God has established His throne on high to look across the earth and judge people accordingly. Wicked nations and enemies of the Israelites were overthrown and cut off in the past. Those nations are not even remembered today, but Israel lives on. The Lord will continue to do this for Israel, and He will live on beyond the memory of any of us. He will judge us and minister justice at the end of time. Verse 8 is a prophecy of that. However, we can also expect justice on earth.

Verse 9 says that God is our high tower. A high tower was a place where the enemy didn't have access, but it was also a watchtower where God Himself would detect the coming of the enemy at a distance. Those who are oppressed, destitute, and desperate can count on Him. If we know God personally, not just of Him but have experienced his mercy, we can lean all our weight on Him (vs. 10). We can trust Him completely because He has not, nor will He forsake

10 And they who know Your name [who have experience and acquaintance with Your mercy] will lean on and confidently put their trust in You, for You, Lord, have not forsaken those who seek (inquire of and for) You [on the authority of God's Word and the right of their necessity].
11 Sing praises to the Lord, Who dwells in Zion! Declare among the peoples His doings!
12 For He Who avenges the blood [of His people shed unjustly] remembers them; He does not forget the cry of the afflicted (the poor and the humble).
13 Have mercy upon me and be gracious to me, O Lord; consider how I am afflicted by those who hate me, You Who lift me up from the gates of death,
14 That I may show forth (recount and tell aloud) all Your praises! In the gates of the Daughter of Zion I will rejoice in Your salvation and Your saving help.
15 The nations have sunk down in the pit that they made; in the net which they hid is their own foot caught.
16 The Lord has made Himself known; He executes judgment; the wicked are snared in the work of their own hands. Higgaion [meditation]. Selah [pause, and calmly think of that]!

those who seek after Him and make Him their authority (Deuteronomy 31:8).

David breaks into praise again in verse 11 and encourages all who listen to this song to declare loudly God's doings. What has and will God do? He will pay back for unjust bloodshed, and He remembers the hurt and prayers of the poor and humble (vs. 12). He has mercy on us and lifts us up out of death into glorious light (vs. 13). He offers us salvation and brings us help (vs. 14). He will turn back the wicked (vs. 16). He will meet the expectations of the meek and take care of the poor (vs.18). He will not let men prevail over Him or His people (Israelites and Christians vs. 9)

Wow! Let us rejoice and sing praises because of what the Lord has done and will continue to do! I encourage your prayer for Psalm 8 to be a long list of "Thank Yous." Thank Him for the big things and thank Him for the small, seemingly insignificant things. Thank Him for everything in between, and then go out and share what He has done in your life.

Use this space to write a list of everything you are thankful for, even small things like your cozy bed and dishwasher...

17 The wicked shall be turned back [headlong into premature death] into Sheol (the place of the departed spirits of the wicked), even all the nations that forget or are forgetful of God.
18 For the needy shall not always be forgotten, and the expectation and hope of the meek and the poor shall not perish forever.
19 Arise, O Lord! Let not man prevail; let the nations be judged before You.
20 Put them in fear [make them realize their frail nature], O Lord, that the nations may know themselves to be but men. Selah [pause, and calmly think of that]!

Side Note: cdc.gov, m.christianpost.com, and dosomething.org

There are so many bad things in the news…

1. There were over 20,000 murders in the US in 2020.
2. In the first eight months of 2014, ISIS and related groups killed over 8,400 Iraqi civilians, injured over 15,700, had taken hundreds as slaves, and displaced thousands from their homes.
3. More than 3 billion people live on less than $2.50 a day. 1 billion children worldwide are living in poverty, and 22,000 children die each day due to poverty.

The point is not to focus on the bad but to pray about it and be thankful for what you have.

Prayer: Lord, I praise you and rejoice because you have been so good to me. I am thankful for my salvation and your mercy and grace. I am thankful for your righteous judgments. Thank you for remembering me and hearing me. I praise you because you are my hope, and you won't let me down. Thank you for my _____, _____, _____ (Be specific and write down a detailed list. Add to the list anytime a prayer is answered, or you are blessed by God in big or small ways. Return to the list regularly to remind you how great God is, so you can rejoice like David did in this Psalm).

Week 9 Day 1 Notes for Psalm 9: Which verse stood out to you the most and why?

_____

_____

_____

_____

What important life lesson can you apply from this Psalm?

_____

_____

_____

Week 9 Day 2 Devotions: Reread Psalm 9:1-2 and the following verses on praising and thanking God.

Psalm 100:1-5 *Shout joyfully to the LORD, all the earth. Serve the LORD with gladness and delight; Come before His presence with joyful singing. Know and fully recognize with gratitude that the LORD Himself is God; It is He who has made us, not we ourselves [and we are His]. We are His people and the sheep of His pasture. Enter His gates with a song of thanksgiving And His courts with praise. Be thankful to Him, bless and praise His name. For the LORD is good; His mercy and lovingkindness are everlasting, His faithfulness [endures] to all generations.*

1 Chronicles 29:12-13 *Both riches and honor come from You, and You rule over all. In Your hand is power and might; and it is in Your hands to make great and to give strength to everyone. Now therefore, our God, we thank You, and praise Your glorious name.*

1 Thessalonians 5:18 *in every situation [no matter what the circumstances] be thankful and continually give thanks to God; for this is the will of God for you in Christ Jesus.*

When are we supposed to praise God? _____

For what is He being praised in Psalm 100 and 1 Chronicles (there's at least 10 things listed)?

_____

_____

_____

_____

Revisit your list of thanks from your prayer for day 1.

Week 9 Day 3 Devotions: Reread Psalm 9:1 and the following verses on telling about God's good deeds.

Mark 5:19 *Jesus did not let him [come], but [instead] He said to him, "Go home to your family and tell them all the great things that the Lord has done for you, and how He has had mercy on you."*

Daniel 4:2 *It has seemed good to me to declare the signs and wonders which the Most High God has done for me.*

Psalm 78:4-8 *We will not hide them from their children, But [we will] tell to the generation to come the praiseworthy deeds of the LORD, And [tell of] His great might and power and the wonderful works that He has done. ⁵ For He established a testimony (a specific precept) in Jacob And appointed a law in Israel, Which He commanded our fathers That they should teach to their children [the great facts of God's transactions with Israel], ⁶ That the generation to come might know them, that the children still to be born May arise and recount them to their children, ⁷ That they should place their confidence in God And not forget the works of God, But keep His commandments, ⁸ And not be like their fathers—A stubborn and rebellious generation, A generation that did not prepare its heart to know and follow God, And whose spirit was not faithful to God.*

Based on Psalm 78:6-8 why should you tell others, especially children, about God's wonderful works?

_____

_____

_____

_____

Week 9 Day 4 Devotions: Reread Psalm 9: 4-6 and the following verses on how God takes care of enemies and nations.

Leviticus 26:4, 6-7 *If you walk in My statutes and keep My commandments and [obediently] do them...I will also grant peace in the land, so that you may lie down and there will be no one to make you afraid. I will also eliminate harmful animals from the land, and no sword will pass through your land. And you will chase your enemies, and they will fall before you by the sword.*

Deuteronomy 9:5 *It is not for your righteousness or for the uprightness of your heart that you are going to possess their land, but because of the wickedness of these nations the LORD your God is driving them out before you, and to confirm the oath which the LORD swore to your fathers, to Abraham, Isaac, and Jacob.*

Isaiah 60:12 *"For the nation or the kingdom which will not serve you [Jerusalem] shall perish, and the nations [that refuse to serve] shall be utterly ruined."*

Some people use Old Testament passages about God commanding the Israelites to wipe out cities completely to say that He is not just or good. Those examples must be taken in context Biblically and historically. What reason is given for nations being destroyed in Deuteronomy 9 and Isaiah 60?

_____

_____

What did God promise for those who listen to His commands in Leviticus 26?

_____

_____

God has given everyone a chance to follow Him, even the nations of the Old Testament. Now we have the hope of salvation through Jesus' death on the cross. Using these (and other) verses and concepts what could you say to someone who feels there's a discrepancy?

_____

_____

_____

Week 9 Day 5 Devotions: Reread Psalm 9:7 and the following verse on God reigning forever.

Exodus 15:18 *"The LORD shall reign to eternity and beyond."*

Daniel 4:3 *"How great are His signs And how mighty are His wonders! His kingdom is an everlasting kingdom and His dominion is from generation to generation.*

Revelation 11:15 *Then the seventh angel sounded [his trumpet]; and there were loud voices in heaven, saying, "The kingdom (dominion, rule) of the world has become the kingdom of our Lord and of His Christ; and He will reign forever and ever."*

Imagine what it will be like when we are finally ruled by God instead of man. Briefly describe the differences.

_____

_____

Week 9 Day 6 Devotions: Reread Psalm 9:10 and the following verses on knowing God's name. Please visit the following website to learn a few of the names of God and see the references for them. Then write down your top 2 favorite names, what they mean, and why they are your favorite. https://www.blueletterbible.org/study/misc/name_god.cfm

1. _____

_____

_____

2. _____

_____

_____

Week 9 Day 7 Devotions: Reread Psalm 9:15-16 and the following verses on falling into your own trap.

Proverbs 28:10 *He who leads the upright astray on an evil path Will himself fall into his own pit, but the blameless will inherit good.*

Ecclesiastes 10:8 *He who digs a pit [for others] may fall into it, and a serpent may bite him who breaks through a [stone] wall.*

Esther 7:10 *So they hanged Haman on the gallows that he had prepared for Mordecai. Then the king's anger subsided.*

What is one way, based on Proverbs 28, that people dig pits for others?

_____

_____

What ways do people lead others astray?

_____

_____

Week 10 Day 1: Psalm 10

¹ Why do You stand afar off, O Lord? Why do You hide Yourself, [veiling Your eyes] in times of trouble (distress and desperation)?
² The wicked in pride and arrogance hotly pursue and persecute the poor; let them be taken in the schemes which they have devised.
³ For the wicked man boasts (sings the praises) of his own heart's desire, and the one greedy for gain curses and spurns, yes, renounces and despises the Lord.
⁴ The wicked one in the pride of his countenance will not seek, inquire for, and yearn for God; all his thoughts are that there is no God [so He never punishes].
⁵ His ways are grievous [or persist] at all times; Your judgments [Lord] are far above and on high out of his sight [so he never thinks about them]; as for all his foes, he sniffs and sneers at them.
⁶ He thinks in his heart, I shall not be moved; for throughout all generations I shall not come to want or be in adversity.
⁷ His mouth is full of cursing, deceit, oppression (fraud); under his tongue are trouble and sin (mischief and iniquity).
⁸ He sits in ambush in the villages; in hiding places he slays the innocent; he watches

Though David is credited with writing most of the Psalms, several other authors are also included in this book. It is a unique book in the Bible in that multiple authors' works from several different time periods are compiled here. Many believe that David wrote this Psalm as a continuation of Psalm 9. However, there is not enough concrete evidence to prove this. There are also no instructions before the Psalm as to the type of music the Psalm is to be sung to. No matter who the author or the exact context in which this Psalm was written, we believe as Christians that God watches over His Word so that it is not added to or subtracted from by man. (Jeremiah 1:12 and Revelation 22:19). We believe that the Holy Spirit guided the writers and those compiling those writings into one book (2 Timothy 3:16). Thus, we believe that we can trust the Word to be true and poignant to our lives today. We especially need this assurance during troubled times.

During a crisis, it can feel as though you are in the vortex of a violent swirling tornado. Everything becomes dark and hope is stripped away like bark from a tree. Your protective covering seems to be gone and you are vulnerable to your imaginations and to the enemy. It feels as if God has deserted you or, at the very least, He is obscured from your view because the problem is "in your face" day and night. This is where we find our Psalmist in chapter 10 verse one. Sometimes our tornado is caused by wrong choices that we make, and sometimes it is just life slapping us in the face. In this case, however, our Psalmist is vexed by prideful arrogant people who devised schemes against the poor and vulnerable (vs. 2). These people boast about themselves and curse God (vs. 3).

In verse 4 we learn what pride does to a person's heart. Pride keeps us from seeking after our heavenly Father. Pride causes us to be self-reliant because of arrogance; therefore, we, like the men the Psalmist is talking about, can come to a point where we do not even believe God exists. At the very least a prideful person will dismiss God and say to himself, "I can do what I want whenever and however I want. I have prospered for so long because God has hidden His face. He

stealthily for the poor (the helpless and unfortunate).
⁹ He lurks in secret places like a lion in his thicket; he lies in wait that he may seize the poor (the helpless and the unfortunate); he seizes the poor when he draws him into his net.
¹⁰ [The prey] is crushed, sinks down; and the helpless falls by his mighty [claws].
¹¹ [The foe] thinks in his heart, God has quite forgotten; He has hidden His face; He will never see [my deed].
¹² Arise, O Lord! O God, lift up Your hand; forget not the humble [patient and crushed].
¹³ Why does the wicked [man] condemn (spurn and renounce) God? Why has he thought in his heart, You will not call to account?
¹⁴ You have seen it; yes, You note trouble and grief (vexation) to requite it with Your hand. The unfortunate commits himself to You; You are the helper of the fatherless.
¹⁵ Break the arm of the wicked man; and as for the evil man, search out his wickedness until You find no more.
¹⁶ The Lord is King forever and ever; the nations will perish out of His land.
¹⁷ O Lord, You have heard the desire and the longing of the humble and oppressed; You will prepare and strengthen and direct their hearts, You will cause Your ear to hear,

can't see me. He forgets his promises and won't hold me to them" (vs.5,6,11).

Look around our schools, your workplace, and our "Christian" nation. You will see this type of person is becoming more and more prevalent. Atheists, scientists, government officials, pop stars and more are becoming bolder in their disdain for God and his Word. Pride has taken over their hearts and is separating them from Him. They think they are fine without God, and they seem to be prospering despite all of this. We know better though, don't we? We have already learned from previous Psalms that God is just and will judge righteously. He doesn't forget or hide Himself.

This particular breed of person, of whom the Psalmist writes, is not only prideful but is downright evil. Look at verses 7-10 and 13. He curses, lies, commits fraud, and causes trouble. He is sneaky and tries to hurt those he deems to be beneath him and those who are helpless and unfortunate. He lures people into traps of deceit, fraud, and sin in order to destroy them. Finally, he hates God, rejects Him, and thinks himself untouchable.

Our Psalmist calls upon God to make Himself known, to remember His promises, and to move on behalf of those who are oppressed (vs. 12). He believes that God has seen the evil and that He has taken note of the trouble and grief. He knows that those who humble themselves and commit to God will be helped. The same is true for you too. You can remind God of promises from His Word and trust that His Word will not return void (Isaiah 55:11). You should call to Him on behalf of yourself and the lives of others, our nation's leaders and the oppressed.

I have felt like God couldn't see me before. I have felt separated from His view by life's storms, but I was so wrong. I committed to Him and completely stood on His word even though I couldn't understand why this was happening or see a way out. I was forced to see with my heart, and I began to see Him again as I read scriptures (especially the Psalms), listened to Christian music, and listened to good preaching. He also spoke and revealed Himself through godly family members

[18] To do justice to the fatherless and the oppressed, so that man, who is of the earth, may not terrify them anymore.

Side Note:

thefatherlessgeneration. wordpress.com

1. 24 million children in the US (34 percent) live absent their biological father. Nearly 20 million children (27 percent) live in single-parent homes.
2. 63% of youth suicides are from fatherless homes
3. 85% of all children who show behavior disorders come from fatherless homes.
4. 71% of all high school dropouts come from fatherless homes.

and friends. He was there the whole time. I just had to seek Him, trust Him, and rely on Him completely for everything until the swirling stopped and light peeked through the clouds.

God will send evil running and break the enemy's arm so he can't hurt you (vs. 15-16). He will hear and respond. He will prepare, strengthen, and direct your heart if you let Him, and He will speak to you if you will open your heart to Him (vs. 17). He especially helps the fatherless so that men cannot terrify them anymore (vs. 14, 18 also see side note to see the negative effects of fatherlessness).

You may find yourself in this category. Maybe you were put up for adoption and don't know your birth father. Maybe your father ran out on you or has died. In some cases, fathers are abusive or betray their children. Whatever the reason, know that God loves you and sees your hurt. He longs to help you and become your father. I can't think of a better replacement than Him!

Prayer: God, when I can't see you with my eyes or feel your presence, let me remember who you are. Help me to see you and hear you through the many ways you reveal yourself. Thank you for being my father and helper. Thank you for hearing me and strengthening my heart. I am not afraid of evil people because I know they are in your mighty hands. Amen

Week 10 Day 1 Notes for Psalm 10: Which verse stood out to you the most and why?

_____

_____

_____

_____

What important life lesson can you apply from this Psalm?

_____

_____

_____

Week 10 Day 2 Devotions: Reread Psalm 10:2 and the following verses on persecution.

2 Timothy 3:12 *Indeed, all who delight in pursuing righteousness and are determined to live godly lives in Christ Jesus will be hunted and persecuted [because of their faith].*

John 15:18 *"If the world hates you [and it does], know that it has hated Me before it hated you.*

Matthew 5:44 *"But I say to you, love [that is, unselfishly seek the best or higher good for] your enemies and pray for those who persecute you,*

Most people do not want to be hated or persecuted. What do 2 Tim 3 and John 15 tell you about these two topics?

_____

_____

_____

What is your response supposed to be according to Matt 5? _____

Think of an enemy you have now or have had in the past and write a one sentence prayer for them.

_____

_____

_____

Week 10 Day 3 Devotions: Reread Psalm 10: 3-7 and the following verses on people who despise God and think they'll never get caught or punished.

Numbers 32:23 *But if you do not do this, behold, you will have sinned against the LORD; and be sure that your sin will find you out.*

Romans 6:23 *For the wages of sin is death, but the free gift of God [that is, His remarkable, overwhelming gift of grace to believers] is eternal life in Christ Jesus our Lord.*

John 3:19-22 *This is the judgment [that is, the cause for indictment, the test by which people are judged, the basis for the sentence]: the Light has come into the world, and people loved the darkness rather than the Light, for their deeds were evil. For every wrongdoer hates the Light, and does not come to the Light [but shrinks from it] for fear that his [sinful, worthless] activities will be exposed and condemned. But whoever practices truth [and does what is right—morally, ethically, spiritually] comes to the Light, so that his works may be plainly shown to be what they are—accomplished in God [divinely prompted, done with God's help, in dependence on Him]."*

Based on John 3, why to wrongdoers hate and hide from God?

_____

_____

How do Numbers 32 and Romans 6 contrast with what the wicked men think in Psalms 10:3-7?

_____

_____

_____

_____

Week 10 Day 4 Devotions: Reread Psalm 10:12 and the following verses about God arising.

Psalm 68:1 _Let God arise, and His enemies be scattered; Let those who hate Him flee before Him._

Isaiah 31:2 _Yet He is also wise and will bring disaster, and does not retract His words, but will arise against the house of evildoers and against the helpers of those who do evil._

Isaiah 60:1-2 _"Arise [from spiritual depression to a new life], shine [be radiant with the glory and brilliance of the LORD]; for your light has come, And the glory and brilliance of the LORD has risen upon you. "For in fact, darkness will cover the earth and deep darkness will cover the peoples; But the LORD will rise upon you [Jerusalem] And His glory and brilliance will be seen on you._

According to Psalm 68 and Isaiah 31, what will God do to evil people, enemies, and haters?

_____

_____

Isaiah 60 is a prophecy about God rising up for Israel in the end times, but it also tells believers to arise. Based on this verse, what should you arise from and why should you arise?

_____

_____

Week 10 Day 5 Devotions: Reread Psalm 10:14 and the following verses on God seeing and helping us.

Psalm 33:13 _The LORD looks [down] from heaven; He sees all the sons of man;_

Psalm 46:1 _God is our refuge and strength [mighty and impenetrable], A very present and well-proved help in trouble._

Hebrews 13:5-6 *Let your character [your moral essence, your inner nature] be free from the love of money [shun greed—be financially ethical], being content with what you have; for He has said, "I* WILL NEVER *[under any circumstances]* DESERT YOU *[nor give you up nor leave you without support, nor will I in any degree leave you helpless],* NOR WILL I FORSAKE *or* LET YOU DOWN *or* RELAX MY HOLD ON YOU *[assuredly not]!"* [6] *So we take comfort and are encouraged and confidently say, "*THE LORD IS MY HELPER *[in time of need], I* WILL NOT BE AFRAID. WHAT WILL MAN DO TO ME?"*

What promises do you see in the verses above?

_____

_____

_____

_____

Write down a specific thing that you need God's help with *today*, as well as something you need help with either in the *future* or *continuously* (*daily*). Give it to him and trust the promises from the verses above.

_____

_____

_____

Week 10 Day 6 Devotions: Reread psalm 10:16 and the following verses on God as King forever and the wicked being removed.

Lamentations 5:19 *But You, O LORD, reign forever; Your throne endures from generation to [all] generations.*

Daniel 6:26 *I issue a decree that in all the dominion of my kingdom men are to [reverently] fear and tremble before the God of Daniel, For He is the living God, enduring and steadfast forever, And His kingdom is one which will not be destroyed, And His dominion will be forever.*

Proverbs 2:22 *But the wicked will be cut off from the land and the treacherous shall be [forcibly] uprooted and removed from it.*

What comfort do you personally receive from knowing that God reigns forever, and evil will be "uprooted and removed" once and for all?

_____

_____

_____

_____

Week 10 Day 7 Devotions: Reread Psalm 10:18 and the following verses on God's vindication for the fatherless and oppressed.

Romans 12:19 *Beloved, never avenge yourselves, but leave the way open for God's wrath [and His judicial righteousness]; for it is written [in Scripture], "VENGEANCE IS MINE, I WILL REPAY," says the Lord.*

Proverbs 22:22-23 *Do not rob the poor because he is poor [and defenseless], Nor crush the afflicted [by legal proceedings] at the gate [where the city court is held], For the LORD will plead their case
And take the life of those who rob them.*

Deuteronomy 10:18 *He executes justice for the orphan and the widow, and shows His love for the stranger (resident alien, foreigner) by giving him food and clothing.*

List at least 3 things that these verses assure you God will do (there are 5)

_____

_____

_____

_____

Week 11 Day 1: Psalm 11

¹ *In the Lord I take refuge [and put my trust]; how can you say to me, Flee like a bird to your mountain?*
² *For see, the wicked are bending the bow; they make ready their arrow upon the string, that they [furtively] in darkness may shoot at the upright in heart.*
³ *If the foundations are destroyed, what can the [unyieldingly] righteous do, or what has He [the Righteous One] wrought or accomplished?*
⁴ *The Lord is in His holy temple; the Lord's throne is in heaven. His eyes behold; His eyelids test and prove the children of men.*
⁵ *The Lord tests and proves the [unyieldingly] righteous, but His soul abhors the wicked and him who loves violence.*
⁶ *Upon the wicked He will rain quick burning coals or snares; fire, brimstone, and a [dreadful] scorching wind shall be the portion of their cup.*
⁷ *For the Lord is [rigidly] righteous, He loves righteous deeds; the upright shall behold His face, or He beholds the upright.*

Side Note: wallbuilders.com and npr.org

1. "Suppose a nation in some distant region should take the Bible for their

David worked in the court of King Saul for a time, but Saul was prone to fits of rage. David seemed to take the brunt of much of Saul's mental instability. It is thought that Psalm 11 was written during one of Saul's attempts on David's life. David is responding to his friends who have advised him to flee the city (vs. 1). They have told him that evil people have prepared their weapons so they could kill David in the secrecy and darkness of night (vs. 2). His friends meant well and wanted to protect him, but David decided to stay.

He responded by asking them two questions, one in verse 1 and the other in verse 3. First, David asked them how in the world he could run away when he had so firmly placed his trust in God. Then he asked them what the righteous could do if the foundations were destroyed. David could be talking here about the morals of the society under Saul's rule; after all, he has in past Psalms and will continue to speak of wicked men who hurt people and dismiss God. He could also be talking about the crumbling foundation of the actual government due to Saul and others who are leading the nation down a dangerous path.

Though we don't know exactly what the context of verse 3 is, I think what is most important to focus on is the answer to the question: "What do we do if our foundation is destroyed?" We live in a time where our nation is falling away from its Christian foundation. The founding fathers very clearly stated their belief in God, quoted Scripture, and prayed openly and regularly (see side note). Decisions have been made since the 1960s that have chipped away at the biblical principles upon which our society has rested (see side note). This, along with increasing crime rates, extreme random acts of violence, and war breaking out in the Middle East and Europe is enough to weaken the knees of even strong believers.

Besides national security issues, Supreme Court decisions, and terrorist activity abroad, there are many things that can come against us daily to try to destroy our foundation. This could be the foundation of security which comes from having good health or a good job. Our foundation could be emotional stability, which comes from good relationships and blessings in our lives. It could possibly be our very core

only law book and every member should regulate his conduct by the precepts there exhibited... What a Eutopia – what a Paradise would this region be!" John Adams

2. "In the chain of human events, the birthday of the nation is indissolubly linked with the birthday of the Savior. The Declaration of Independence laid the cornerstone of human government upon the first precepts of Christianity." John Quincy Adams

3. "Had the people, during the Revolution, had a suspicion of any attempt to war against Christianity, that Revolution would have been strangled in its cradle... In this age, there can be no substitute for Christianity... That was the religion of the founders of the republic, and they expected it to remain the religion of their descendants." *Congress, U. S. House Judiciary Committee, 1854*

4. *Engel v. Vitale* (1962) and *Abington School District v. Schempp* (1963), the US Supreme Court established what is now the current prohibition on state-sponsored prayer in schools.

beliefs about life and God that are being shaken. So, what do we as Christians do when the solid ground we are standing on crumbles beneath us?

We first take refuge in God (vs. 1) and acknowledge that He is on the throne (vs. 4). We then remind ourselves that He sees everything (vs. 4) and He is our foundation. The foundation of any building is the first part of design. Depending on the type and size of the building, what kind of ground it will stand on, and any natural forces in the area that may affect it, will determine the type of foundation it needs. The deeper and wider the footings, the more stable the building will be. Isaiah 28:16 tells us that God himself laid a sure foundation in Zion (Zion represents God's kingdom literally on Earth and His heavenly kingdom depending on the context). In Matthew 7:24-27 Jesus talked about His words being a firm foundation of rocks versus sand to build our life on. As we build on Jesus and the principles from the Bible, we can stand firm as storms come and waters rise.

After we have done what David has done in verses 1 and 4, we should pray and ask for wisdom, discernment, and the truth about the situation we are facing. Wisdom is the ability to judge correctly and to follow the best course of action based on knowledge and understanding. Discernment is the ability to decide between truth and error, right and wrong. It is the process of making careful distinctions in our thinking about truth.

Sometimes God is testing us to prove our obedience or develop our character (vs. 5), but sometimes what tries to destroy us is a flat-out attack from Satan. Either way our job is to trust God, pray, stay faithful, and learn from the situation. Why should we stay faithful? Because verses 5 and 6 tell us that God will not let evil win. He will punish evil, and those people who practice evil will spend eternity in fire and brimstone if they don't repent.

Finally, David ends Psalm 11 by reminding us once again that God is rigidly righteous. He does not change or bend, so we can trust Him to follow through on His promises and trust Him to be just. One of those promises is in the last lines of verse 7. The people who are in right

5. Since *Roe v. Wade*, (1973), allowed abortion, over 63 million abortions have been performed in the US.
6. In *Stone v. Graham* (1980) the Supreme Court held that the Kentucky's statute that required the Ten Commandments to be posted in school classrooms was in violation of the First Amendment
7. The U.S. Supreme Court's decision in Obergefell vs. Hodges means that same-sex marriage is legal nationwide (2015).

standing with God will see His face and will spend eternity in Heaven with Him. In the meantime, He is beholding us, looking at us with interest and for a purpose (usually indicating the careful observation of details- <u>Vine's Greek Dictionary</u>). How wonderful to know that God, though on his heavenly throne, is looking upon each of us and loves us as His children!

Prayer: Father, I have made you my firm foundation. I have made you my refuge and I will not fear when Satan comes against me. I pray that you will once again be this nation's foundation as government leaders turn back to you. I pray for them and all those in the public eye to repent so they will not experience your eternal and fiery judgment. Thank you for your faithfulness and your righteousness, God. Amen

Week 11 Day 1 Notes for Psalm 11: Which verse stood out to you the most and why?

_____

_____

_____

_____

What important life lesson can you apply from this Psalm?

_____

_____

_____

_____

Week 11 Day 2 Devotions: Reread psalm 11: 3 and the following verses about foundations and lawlessness.

1 John 3:4 ⁴ *Everyone who practices sin also practices lawlessness; and sin is lawlessness [ignoring God's law by action or neglect or by tolerating wrongdoing—being unrestrained by His commands and His will].*

2 Corinthians 6:14 *Do not be unequally bound together with unbelievers [do not make mismatched alliances with them, inconsistent with your faith]. For what partnership can righteousness have with lawlessness? Or what fellowship can light have with darkness?*

Luke 6:47-49 *Everyone who comes to Me and listens to My words and obeys them, I will show you whom he is like: he is like a [far-sighted, practical, and sensible] man building a house, who dug deep and laid a foundation on the rock; and when a flood occurred, the torrent burst against that house and yet could not shake it, because it had been securely built and founded on the rock. But the one who has [merely]heard and has not practiced [what I say], is like a [foolish]man who built a house on the ground without any foundation, and the torrent burst against it; and it immediately collapsed, and the ruin of that house was great."*

According to Luke 6, how is a good, strong foundation formed?

_____

_____

Societal foundations are formed in the same way. Your personal foundation and the foundation of society will fall due to lawlessness. What do 1 John 3 and 2 Corinthians 6 say about lawlessness?

_____

_____

_____

What is something specific you can do today to build a strong foundation?

_____

_____

Week 11 Day 3 Devotions: Reread psalm 11:4 and the following verses about God's throne and holy temple.

1 Kings 22:19 *Micaiah said, "Therefore, hear the word of the LORD. I saw the LORD sitting on His throne, and all the host (army) of heaven standing by Him on His right hand and on His left.*

Daniel 7:9 *"I kept looking Until thrones were set up, And the Ancient of Days (God) took His seat; His garment was white as snow And the hair of His head like pure wool. His throne was flames of fire; Its wheels were a burning fire.*

Isaiah 6:1 *In the year that King Uzziah died, I saw [in a vision] the Lord sitting on a throne, high and exalted, with the train of His royal robe filling the [most holy part of the] temple.*

As you read each scripture through slowly, close your eyes and picture the throne of God. Describe in your own words what God's throne looks like.

_____

_____

_____

_____

Describe how you think you will feel and react when you see God sitting in His holy temple exalted and literally glowing brilliantly with glory.

_____

_____

_____

_____

Week 11 Day 4 Devotions: Reread Psalm 11:5 and the following verses about how God tests man.

Deuteronomy 8:2 *And you shall remember [always] all the ways which the LORD your God has led you these forty years in the wilderness, so that He might humble you and test you, to know what was in your heart (mind), whether you would keep His commandments or not.*

Jeremiah 17:10 *"I, the LORD, search and examine the mind, I test the heart, to give to each man according to his ways, According to the results of his deeds.*

Proverbs 17:3 *The refining pot is for silver and the furnace for gold, But the LORD tests hearts.*

Isaiah 48:10 "Indeed, I have refined you, but not as silver; I have tested and chosen you in the furnace of affliction.

Why does God test us according to Deuteronomy 8 and Jeremiah 17?

_____

_____

_____

Silver must be heated in order to purify it. God "heats" us up too in order to refine us. Sometimes He will allow affliction to test us. In what ways has God used something bad in your life to refine you?

Name the situation and how you came out better and closer to God.

_____

_____

_____

_____

Week 11 Day 5 Devotions: Reread Psalm 11:6 and the following verses about hell.

Matthew 25:41 *"Then He will say to those on His left, 'Leave Me, you cursed ones, into the eternal fire which has been prepared for the devil and his angels (demons);*

Revelation 20:10 *And the devil who had deceived them was hurled into the lake of fire and burning brimstone (sulfur), where the beast (Antichrist) and false prophet are also; and they will be tormented day and night, forever and ever.*

Matthew 13:40-42 *So just as the weeds are gathered up and burned in the fire, so will it be at the end of the age. [41] The Son of Man will send out His angels, and they will gather out of His kingdom all things that offend [those things by which people are led into sin], and all who practice evil [leading others into sin],[42] and will throw them into the furnace of fire; in that place there will be weeping [over sorrow and pain] and grinding of teeth [over distress and anger].*

Just as you closed your eyes and pictured heaven, read these verses slowly and picture what hell will really be like and describe it in your own words.

_____

_____

_____

_____

Write the name of a family member, friend, co-worker, and enemy who is headed for this eternal torment.

_____

Write a brief prayer for their salvation.

_____

_____

_____

_____

Week 11 Day 6 Devotions: Reread psalm 11:7 and the following verses about God's righteousness.

Deuteronomy 32:4 *"The Rock! His work is perfect, For all His ways are just; A God of faithfulness without iniquity (injustice), Just and upright is He.*

Isaiah 51:8 *"For the moth will eat them like a garment, and the worm will eat them like wool. But My righteousness and justice [faithfully promised] will exist forever, and My salvation to all generations."*

Jeremiah 9:24 *but let the one who boasts boast in this, that he understands and knows Me [and acknowledges Me and honors Me as God and recognizes without any doubt], that I am the LORD who practices lovingkindness, justice and righteousness on the earth, for in these things I delight," says the LORD.*

Write down every description about God that you can find in the verses above (There's at least 7).

_____

_____

_____

Circle the description that means the most to you. Write down why it is important to you and praise Him for it now.

_____

_____

_____

Week 11 Day 7 Devotions: Reread psalm 11:7 and the following verses about seeing God's face

Matthew 5:8 *"Blessed [anticipating God's presence, spiritually mature] are the pure in heart [those with integrity, moral courage, and godly character], for they will see God.*

Hebrews 12:14 *Continually pursue peace with everyone, and the sanctification without which no one will [ever] see the Lord.*

Revelation 1:7 *BEHOLD, HE IS COMING WITH THE CLOUDS, and every eye will see Him, even those who pierced Him; and all the tribes (nations) of the earth will mourn over Him [realizing their sin and guilt, and anticipating the coming wrath]. So it is to be. Amen.*

Who will see God based on these 3 verses?

_____

_____

_____

Those who are saved will rejoice when they see God, but what will others feel who have rejected Him?

_____

_____

_____

Week 12 Day 1: Psalm 12

¹ Help, Lord! For principled and godly people are here no more; faithfulness and the faithful vanish from among the sons of men.
² To his neighbor each one speaks words without use or worth or truth; with flattering lips and double heart [deceitfully] they speak.
³ May the Lord cut off all flattering lips and the tongues that speak proud boasting,
⁴ Those who say, With our tongues we prevail; our lips are our own [to command at our will]—who is lord and master over us?
⁵ Now will I arise, says the Lord, because the poor are oppressed, because of the groans of the needy; I will set him in safety and in the salvation for which he pants.
⁶ The words and promises of the Lord are pure words, like silver refined in an earthen furnace, purified seven times over.
⁷ You will keep them and preserve them, O Lord; You will guard and keep us from this [evil] generation forever.
⁸ The wicked walk or prowl about on every side, as vileness is exalted [and baseness is rated high] among the sons of men.

Evil will always be among us as we wait for the second coming of the Lord (1 Thessalonians 4:15-5:4). As we look around the world today, news headings ring out with the effects of Adam and Eve's decision to disobey God over 5,000 years ago and "do their own thing." The consequences of their decision brought sin into a perfectly created paradise, and we are still reaping the consequences in the 21st-century.

It is amazing to me when I read the Psalms that David was experiencing the same thing 2,000 years ago in his society that we are experiencing today. In verse 1 he cries out for help because he has looked around his world for men with godly morals, faithfulness, and integrity and cannot find even one. Neighbors, instead of being able to be counted on, are lying to each other, and their commitments are intentionally worthless– merely talk with no actions (vs. 2).

The people David sees prevailing and growing in number say, "Who rules over us? We rule over ourselves because we say so!" (vs. 4). They are full of pride and are double minded (vs. 2, 3). The wicked sneak around and seem to be lurking everywhere waiting to make their move (vs.8). They're inescapable. Finally, he sees that people are actually exalting vileness (vs.8). Exalt means to lift up, esteem highly, or to prize something. Vileness means morally depraved, hateful, and dishonorable. The people in David's time were actually honoring despicable, obscene, and impure behavior.

Can you see how closely related verses 1-4 and 8 are to our society today? Many people, even Christians, do not live by the guidelines and principles set forth in the Bible. Human secularism has invaded our society like cancer metastasizing and has turned the world gray (see side note). We used to have black and white. Sin was sin and we taught that to our children. We posted it on the walls of classrooms and courthouses, talked about it at dinner and with our friends, and even watched TV shows which reinforced biblical morals. Now we have "50 Shades of Gray," and those who follow the "old" rules are considered "old-school," outdated, narrow minded, and even bigoted.

The world craves video games, music, and movies with

Side Note:
Secularhumanism.org

1. It is the belief that "celebrates emancipating the individual from traditional controls by family, church, and state, increasingly empowering each of us to set the terms of his or her own life. Secular humanists hold that ethics is consequential, to be judged by results. This is in contrast to so-called command ethics, in which right and wrong are defined in advance and attributed to divine authority."

2. Silver must be heated to 1760°F in order to melt it and separate it from other metals and impurities.

3. I encourage you to put some kind of protection on all of your electronic devices. I have used K9 Web protection for years. It is free, and you can set your parental controls as strict or lenient as you want. There is a password override in case it blocks a site you wish to have access to.

Prayer: God, I seem to be surrounded by evil and evil is being exulted all around me. Help me to stand firm

violence, cursing, and explicit sexual content. We've gone from Pac-Man to Grand Theft Auto, I Love Lucy to Two and a Half Men, the Beach Boys to Lil Wayne, and Back to the Future 1-3 to Horrible Bosses 1 and 2. These things never would've been allowed 60 years ago but are so prevalent now that even commercials have to be censored or screened by parents who really want to protect their children from filth. Even hamburgers are sold by surgically enhanced women in string bikinis crawling around seductively. Baseness is highly rated in today's world just as it was when David wrote verse 8, and the evil grows with each generation. The Bible even says that it will grow worse and worse until he returns (2 Timothy 3:13).

One problem we face today that David did not is technology. The media and internet have provided a way for even more rubbish to pervade our communities and surrounds us on every side (vs. 8). Too often technology is used to perpetuate sin when controlled by the wrong people. A friend had a quote on his email that said, "He who controls the media rules the world." Media moguls have tried to say that they are just giving people what they want, but I challenge that statement. I believe people would not crave violent and sexual content in music, games, and movies if we would not have fed it to them in the first place. It started off with a seed, a moral boundary pushed here and there on one television show and on one music video. The next year it was a little more prevalent, then more the following year and so forth. These acts were calculated and deliberate in order to desensitize the public and to enlarge the gray areas. Now it is hard to find a TV show or movie that is truly "family friendly" from a biblical standpoint.

So, what can Christians do? We can cry out to God for help like David did in verse 1. Don't back down in your concerns and prayers. Don't allow yourself to be consumed. Keep your biblical principles black and white– don't live in the gray areas. We are to uphold what we know to be true from God's Word. It is okay to call sin "sin," but do it lovingly (Isaiah 5:20, Galatians 5:19-21). We are not called

and follow your Word. Help me to have strong godly principles, to be faithful, and to speak truth in love. Help me to live with integrity and not to be double minded. I pray for this generation to turn back to you. Thank you for guarding us and keeping us safe. Amen.

to judge but are commanded to love (Matthew 7:1, Mark 12:31). We are also to trust that God will keep us safe (vs. 5) and will keep His promises (vs. 6).

As the darkness in the world becomes darker, the light of truth will shine brighter. Those who hold to the truth may find themselves under pressure like they never have in the past, but God promises to guard us and preserve us forever from the evil generation surrounding us (vs.7). David describes God's words as pure, like silver put in a furnace seven times to purify it (see side note). God's promises can be counted on, and unlike those people in verse 2 God is not double minded but is pure and true. Amen!

Week 12 Day 1 Notes for Psalm 12: Which verse stood out to you the most and why?

_____

_____

_____

_____

What important life lesson can you apply from this Psalm?

_____

_____

_____

_____

Week 12 Day 2 Devotions: Reread psalm 12:1 and the following verses on God rescuing us.

Lamentations 3:58 *O Lord, You have pleaded my soul's cause [You have guided my way and protected me]; You have rescued and redeemed my life.*

2 Timothy 4:18 *The Lord will rescue me from every evil assault, and He will bring me safely into His heavenly kingdom; to Him be the glory forever and ever. Amen.*

Galatians 1:4 *who gave Himself [as a sacrifice to atone] for our sins [to save and sanctify us] so that He might rescue us from this present evil age, in accordance with the will and purpose and plan of our God and Father…*

What action words do you see in these verses that God will perform for you (There's at least 7)?

_____

_____

_____

_____

Week 12 Day 3 Devotions: Reread Psalm 12:2-3 and the following verses about liars.

Psalm 63:11 *But the king will rejoice in God; Everyone who swears by Him [honoring the true God, acknowledging His authority and majesty] will glory, For the mouths of those who speak lies will be stopped.*

Revelation 21:8 *But as for the cowards and unbelieving and abominable [who are devoid of character and personal integrity and practice or tolerate immorality], and murderers, and sorcerers [with intoxicating drugs], and idolaters and occultists [who practice and teach false religions], and all the liars [who knowingly deceive and twist truth], their part will be in the lake that blazes with fire and brimstone, which is the second death."*

Colossians 3:9 *Do not lie to one another, for you have stripped off the old self with its evil practices,*

Think of a time when you were lied about. Write their name down _____
Forgiveness is key to God forgiving you and answering your prayer. Pray and forgive the person who lied about you, and release them and the situation to God. Now draw a cross through their name to show that you have forgiven them.

Think of a time when you have hurt someone by lying to or about them. Write their name down and the offense and ask God to forgive you for your offense—be specific.

_____

_____

_____

Week 12 Day 4 Devotions: Reread Psalm 12:5 and the following verses on God arising.

Isaiah 33:10 *"Now I will arise," says the LORD. "Now I will be exalted; now I will be lifted up.*

Numbers 10:35 *Whenever the ark set out, Moses said, "Rise up, O LORD! Let Your enemies be scattered; And let those who hate You flee before You."*

Isaiah 28:21 *For the LORD will rise up as at Mount Perazim, He will be stirred up as in the Valley of Gibeon, To do His work, His unusual and incredible work, And to accomplish His work, His extraordinary work.*

Based on Isaiah 33, what will happen *to* God when He arises?_____

According to Numbers 10 and Isaiah 28, what will happen *because* God arises?

_____

_____

_____

_____

Do you have any "work" that you need God to accomplish in your life today, whether extraordinary or not? Write it down and exalt Him above what needs to be done. Count on Him to arise on your behalf.

_____

_____

_____

_____

Week 12 Day 5 Devotions: Reread Psalm 12:6 and the following verses on God's words being pure.

Proverbs 30:5 *Every word of God is tested and refined [like silver]; He is a shield to those who trust and take refuge in Him.*

John 17:17 *Sanctify them in the truth [set them apart for Your purposes, make them holy]; Your word is truth.*

Revelation 21:5 *And He who sits on the throne said, "Behold, I am making all things new." Also He said, "Write, for these words are faithful and true [they are accurate, incorruptible, and trustworthy]."*

We have seen already that God refines us like silver to make us pure, but He also tests/refines His own Word. Why does He do that?

_____

_____

_____

How does knowing His Word is true make you feel and why?

_____

_____

_____

_____

Week 12 Day 6 Devotions: Reread Psalm 12:7 and the following verses about God preserving/keeping us from evil.

Psalm 121:7 *The LORD will protect you from all evil; He will keep your life.*

Proverbs 19:23 *The fear of the LORD leads to life, So that one may sleep satisfied, untouched by evil.*

2 Timothy 4:18 *The Lord will rescue me from every evil assault, and He will bring me safely into His heavenly kingdom; to Him be the glory forever and ever. Amen.*

There is evil all around us, and you may personally have been touched by evil. Knowing that, how do you reconcile the appearance of a conflict between what you have seen or experienced and what is said in these verses? Hint: focus on 2 Timothy 4 and other concepts you have learned throughout this study.

_____

_____

_____

_____

Week 12 Day 7 Devotions: Reread Psalm 12:8 and the following verses on wickedness and evildoers.

2 Timothy 3:13 *But evil men and impostors will go on from bad to worse, deceiving and being deceived.*

Micah 2:1 *Woe (judgment is coming) to those who devise wickedness And plot evil on their beds! When morning comes, they practice evil Because it is in the power of their hands.*

Psalm 37:1-2 *Do not worry because of evildoers, Nor be envious toward wrongdoers; ² For they will wither quickly like the grass, and fade like the green herb.*

According to 2 Timothy 3, what can we count on happening?

_____

_____

_____

Based on the next 2 verses what can we count on that will happen to evildoers?

_____

_____

_____

Briefly describe something you have personally seen or experienced that you feel was truly evil.

_____

_____

_____

_____

Even when you may not see the end result personally, you can count on the truth of God's Word and it promises that evildoers will wither away and receive judgement. Pray that God will give you the confidence in Him to believe he will take of whatever evil you have experienced and pray for those involved to be changed by the power of the Holy Spirit.

Week 13 Day 1: Psalm 13

¹ How long will You forget me, O Lord? Forever? How long will You hide Your face from me?
² How long must I lay up cares within me and have sorrow in my heart day after day? How long shall my enemy exalt himself over me?
³ Consider and answer me, O Lord my God; lighten the eyes [of my faith to behold Your face in the pitch like darkness], lest I sleep the sleep of death,
⁴ Lest my enemy say, I have prevailed over him, and those that trouble me rejoice when I am shaken.
⁵ But I have trusted, leaned on, and been confident in Your mercy and loving-kindness; my heart shall rejoice and be in high spirits in Your salvation.
⁶ I will sing to the Lord, because He has dealt bountifully with me.

Side Note:

Saul tried to kill David a dozen times, and David was on the run from Saul for over 12 years in desserts, mountains, and caves.

Prayer: God, your loving kindness and your mercy bring me joy. No matter what life throws at me I know that

Imagine that you have served God your whole life. You have personally experienced His presence, and His strength has filled and overtaken you. You have slain a bear and a lion with your bare hands while tending sheep and a great giant who made an entire army quiver with the sound of his voice. Imagine that God himself called you to be king over his chosen people. You have been honored, set apart by His mighty hand. You should be in the palace dining with your friends and family and being entertained with beautiful music. Yet, where are you? Where do you, brave shepherd and future King, find yourself?

If you were David, you would find yourself deep in the cave of Adullam exhausted and crying out to God for salvation from your enemy King Saul. You have been running for days from trained soldiers who are hunting you for the king. You are exhausted. You are alone. Deep in the cave it is pitch black and you can't light a fire for fear of being found. Why would such a brave young man and the anointed king run and hide; surely, he hadn't lost faith in God's power to help him? No, that was not it at all. David knew that it was not his place to deal with Saul. He did not want to usurp God's authority and overthrow the current king of Israel. He knew that God would deal with Saul in His own way and His own timing.

It can be difficult to wait on God. Our minds tend to jump into "fix-it "or "figure it out" mode when we find ourselves in a bad situation. Sometimes, like David, we keep having one thing after another come against us and we don't know why God keeps allowing it. Has he forgotten us? Will this trial last forever? David is asking the same questions in verses 1 and 2 that we sometimes ask ourselves when all we see is darkness: "God, can you hear me? Can you see me? Are you even there? How long will my heart hurt? How long until you answer my prayers?"

David asked God to answer him and open his eyes lest he die (vs. 3). What he means by this is that he wants God to open the eyes of his heart so he can see the truth of the situation. If David looked with his physical eyes only, he

I can count on you. Help me to see the blessings that you have provided in my life and to focus on you and the truth of your Word instead of the problems I face. In Jesus name, Amen.

would have laid down and died from lack of hope. If God did not open his heart to see through faith what he knew to be true, then he would be shaken and defeated by his enemies (vs. 4). God must have answered David somewhere in the darkness because he declares that he will rejoice and be in high spirits as he relies on his confidence in God's mercy and love (vs. 5). David, in the cave and on the run, sings to God because God has blessed him abundantly (vs. 6).

In the midst of turmoil, past, present, and future blessings are sometimes impossible to see with our physical eyes. We must see through spiritual eyes of faith and focus on the promise, not the problem. This is easier said than done– trust me, but it is necessary so that despair doesn't overtake you. With spiritual eyes you can fight for your breakthrough in prayer. Sing to the Lord, even though you don't have your answer yet because your heart knows that He is good. Rejoicing in the darkness will give Satan a big kick in the teeth and will bring the light of truth to you so that you can make it through the storm and patiently wait on God for an answer.

Week 13 Day 1 Notes for Psalm 13: Which verse stood out to you the most and why?

_____

_____

_____

_____

What important life lesson can you apply from this Psalm?

_____

_____

_____

_____

Week 13 Day 2 Devotions: Reread Psalm 13:1 and the following verses on God hiding His face.

Isaiah 59:2 *But your wickedness has separated you from your God, And your sins have hidden His face from you so that He does not hear.*

Isaiah 30:20 *Though the Lord gives you the bread of adversity and the water of oppression, yet your Teacher will no longer hide Himself, but your eyes will [constantly] see your Teacher.*

Ezekiel 39:29 *I will not hide My face from them any longer, because I will have poured out My Spirit on the house of Israel," says the Lord GOD.*

In many cases God hides His face due to our _____, according to Isaiah 59. Yet, sometimes He allows us to go through _____ to teach us (Is.30).

Have you ever felt like God has hidden Himself from you? How did that make you feel and what brought you to the other side of that trying time?

_____

_____

_____

_____

If you are currently feeling as David often felt in the Psalms, that God was hidden from Him and not answering prayer, hold on to the hope of His lovingkindness and wait for Him to pour out His Spirit on you—it's coming if you'll trust in Him.

Week 13 Day 3 Devotions: Reread psalm 13:2 and the following verses on sorrow.

Ecclesiastes 3:4 *To everything there is a season… A time to weep and a time to laugh; A time to mourn and a time to dance.*

Psalm 30:5, 11 *For His anger is but for a moment, His favor is for a lifetime. Weeping may endure for a night, But a shout of joy comes in the morning.* [11] *You have turned my mourning into dancing for me; You have taken off my sackcloth and clothed me with joy,*

Revelation 21:4 *and He will wipe away every tear from their eyes; and there will no longer be death; there will no longer be sorrow and anguish, or crying, or pain; for the [a]former order of things has passed away."*

A thought--Had it not been for deep sorrow, I would be unable to know abundant joy. Had it not been for the darkness, I would have no appreciation for the light. Had it not been for the fearful storm, I would have no need for His unexplainable peace. Had it not been for anger and helplessness, I would never have fully understood His tender loving kindness.

Fill in the following blanks with one of your own experiences: Had it not been for _____

_____, I would (not have learned or gained) _____

_____

How do these verses bring you hope?

_____

_____

_____

_____

Week 13 Day 4 Devotions: Reread Psalm 13:3 and the following verses on light, life, and God answering prayer.

Micah 7:8 *Do not rejoice over me [amid my tragedies], O my enemy! Though I fall, I will rise; Though I sit in the darkness [of distress], the LORD is a light for me.*

John 6:63 *It is the Spirit who gives life; the flesh conveys no benefit [it is of no account]. The words I have spoken to you are spirit and life [providing eternal life].*

John 15:7 *If you remain in Me and My words remain in you [that is, if we are vitally united and My message lives in your heart], ask whatever you wish and it will be done for you.*

The Spirit gives you _____. You will have answers to your prayers if you

_____

What prayers are you asking God to hear and answer today?

_____

_____

_____

_____

Week 13 Day 5 Devotions: Reread Psalm 13:5 and the following verses on God's faithfulness and loving kindness.

Deuteronomy 7:9 *Therefore know [without any doubt] and understand that the LORD your God, He is God, the faithful God, who is keeping His covenant and His [steadfast] lovingkindness to a thousand generations with those who love Him and keep His commandments;*

Nehemiah 9:17 *"They refused to listen and obey, And did not remember Your wondrous acts which You had performed among them; So they stiffened their necks and [in their rebellion] appointed a leader in order to return them to slavery in Egypt. But You are a God of forgiveness, Gracious and merciful and compassionate, Slow to anger and abounding in lovingkindness; And You did not abandon them.*

Isaiah 63:7 *I will tell of the loving kindnesses of the Lord, and the praiseworthy deeds of the Lord, According to all that the Lord has done for us, And His great goodness toward the house of Israel, Which He has shown them according to His compassion and according to the abundance of His loving kindnesses.*

Briefly describe 2 specific instances where you were a recipient of God's loving kindness.

_____

_____

_____

_____

_____

_____

Week 13 Day 6 Devotions: Reread Psalm 13:5 and the following verses on rejoicing in God's salvation.

Isaiah 12:2-3 *"Behold, God, my salvation! I will trust and not be afraid, For the Lord God is my strength and song; Yes, He has become my salvation." Therefore with joy you will draw water From the springs of salvation.*

Habakkuk 3:17-19 *Though the fig tree does not blossom And there is no fruit on the vines, Though the yield of the olive fails And the fields produce no food, Though the flock is cut off from the fold And there are no cattle in the stalls, Yet I will [choose to] rejoice in the Lord; I will [choose to] shout in exultation in the [victorious] God of my salvation!*

Philippians 4:4 *Rejoice in the Lord always [delight, take pleasure in Him]; again I will say, rejoice!*

Even in troubled times you have a reason to rejoice. What can bring you joy according to the verses above?

_____

It is easy to have joy when things are going well. List some things you can rejoice about today that remain whether it's a good or bad day.

_____

_____

_____

Week 13 Day 7 Devotions: Reread Psalm 13:6 and the following verses on singing to God.

Psalm 33:1-3 *Rejoice in the Lord, you righteous ones; Praise is becoming and appropriate for those who are upright [in heart—those with moral integrity and godly character]. Give thanks to the Lord with the lyre; Sing* *praises to Him with the harp of ten strings. Sing to Him a new song; Play skillfully [on the strings] with a loud and joyful sound.*

2 Chronicles 5:12-13 *and all of the Levitical singers, Asaph, Heman, and Jeduthun, with their sons and relatives, clothed in fine linen, with cymbals, harps, and lyres were standing at the east end of the altar, and with them a hundred and twenty priests blowing trumpets in unison when the trumpeters and singers were to make themselves heard with one voice praising and thanking the LORD, and when they raised their voices accompanied by the trumpets and cymbals and [other] instruments of music, and when they praised the LORD, saying, "For He is good, for His mercy and lovingkindness endure forever," then the house of the LORD was filled with a cloud,*

Revelation 15:3-4 *And they sang the song of Moses, the bond-servant of God, and the song of the Lamb, saying, "Great and wonderful and awe-inspiring are Your works [in judgment], O Lord God, the Almighty [the Omnipotent, the Ruler of all]; Righteous and true are Your ways, O King of the nations!" "Who will not fear [reverently] and glorify Your name, O Lord [giving You honor and praise in worship]? For You alone are holy; For ALL THE NATIONS SHALL COME AND WORSHIP BEFORE YOU, FOR YOUR RIGHTEOUS ACTS [Your just decrees and judgments] HAVE BEEN REVEALED and DISPLAYED."*

Who should sing based on Psalm 33? _____

What happened when the singers praised the Lord in 2 Chronicles 5?

_____

_____

List some of the characteristics of God that are praised in the song of Revelation 15.

_____

_____

_____

List some of God's characteristics that you personally want to praise Him for today.

_____

_____

Make a point today to listen to some Christian songs and sing your own songs of praise to your God.

Week 14 Day 1: Psalm 14

¹ The [empty-headed] fool has said in his heart, There is no God. They are corrupt, they have done abominable deeds; there is none that does good or right.
² The Lord looked down from heaven upon the children of men to see if there were any who understood, dealt wisely, and sought after God, inquiring for and of Him and requiring Him [of vital necessity].
³ They are all gone aside, they have all together become filthy; there is none that does good or right, no, not one.
⁴ Have all the workers of iniquity no knowledge, who eat up my people as they eat bread and who do not call on the Lord?
⁵ There they shall be in great fear [literally—dreading a dread], for God is with the generation of the [uncompromisingly] righteous (those upright and in right standing with Him).
⁶ You [evildoers] would put to shame and confound the plans of the poor and patient, but the Lord is his safe refuge.
⁷ Oh, that the salvation of Israel would come out of Zion! When the Lord shall restore the fortunes of His people, then Jacob shall rejoice and Israel shall be glad.

In Psalm 8 David sang about God's majesty and how he could see God in the stars. We also know that David felt the presence of God very strongly in his life on many occasions. Not only does he have the Israelites' history as evidence that God exists, he has a personal testimony. Personal testimony is one of the best witnessing tools believers have in their possession. When we open our hearts and share with nonbelievers what we have personally seen, heard, and experienced, we can genuinely touch them. We are also less likely to be argumentative, harsh, or pushy when we share God in this way.

In Psalm 14, David is talking about people who do not believe God exists– atheists. He calls them empty headed fools (vs. 1). It is hard for David to understand how anyone could refuse to believe in the existence of God. David and Christians today rely on scriptures to prove God exists, but quoting the Bible means nothing to atheists because they don't believe it is the Word of God. If they don't believe in God or His Word then how can we reach them? If they see us living a consistent life of integrity, we have a much better chance that they will believe our testimony when we share it with them. After all, a person can't logically argue with what you have personally experienced.

We can use scriptures to explain to them why we live the way we do, why we choose certain activities, and why we stay away from others. It is imperative that we don't live like the world. We are called to be salt and light, but we can't do our job and reach nonbelievers if we look like everyone else (Matthew 5:13-16). Atheists, Buddhists, Muslims, Hindus, Mormons, Jehovah's Witnesses…all need our light to shine bright. We would be just as foolish as they (who don't believe God exists) if we lost our saltiness or hid our light.

As David looks around his city, he tells us that the atheists in his society are corrupt. Not only do they not believe in God, they go against Him and perform abominable deeds. Abominable means repulsive, atrocious, and heinous. That is the problem with removing God from society. If there is no God, then there's no Bible. If there is no Bible, then there are no moral absolutes. If there are no moral absolutes, then

Side Note: free2pray.info

1. Benjamin Franklin-"[Only] a virtuous people are capable of freedom. As nations become corrupt and vicious, they have more need of masters. Whereas true religion and good morals are the only solid foundations of public liberty and happiness… it is hereby earnestly recommended to the several States to take the most effectual measures for the encouragement thereof." Continental Congress, 1778

2. John Adams in a speech to the military in 1798 warned his fellow countrymen stating, "We have no government armed with power capable of contending with human passions unbridled by morality and religion . . . Our Constitution was made only for a moral and religious people. It is wholly inadequate to the government of any other."

Side Note: conservapedia.com

1. Nobel Prize winner Aleksandr Solzhenitsyn was asked to account for the great tragedies that occurred under the brutal communist regime he and fellow citizens suffered under.

people can do whatever they want. They become filthy and move toward sin as a natural tendency (Ps 58:3, Jeremiah 17:9). Society would crumble if not for morals and values that stem from God's Word (see side note).

In verse 2, we see what God truly wants from us. David said God looked down from heaven to see if there were any who understood His purposes and His Word, and He looked for any who used wisdom when making choices and dealing with others. He also wanted to see one more very important thing. Almighty God wanted to see people seeking after Him, learning about Him, and "requiring Him of vital necessity." God longs for us to make Him our lifeline. He loves us so much and wants to have a personal relationship with us (Revelation 3:20, Exodus 25:8, 1 Corinthians 1:9). He designed mankind for this purpose when He created Adam and Eve and walked with them in the garden (Genesis 3:8). Yet, we, His precious creations, have turned against Him (vs. 3) and try to take others down with us (vs. 4).

One day, in the not-so-distant future, mankind will be in great fear for turning their backs on God and corrupting others (2 Thessalonians 1:7-9), but God is with the righteous (vs. 5) and is our safe refuge (vs. 6). Oh, that men would turn their hearts to God and get in right standing with Him before judgment comes!

Let me show you something special about the final verse of Psalm 14. David is literally talking about the salvation of the Israelite people from the current evil people who seem to be overtaking the city. He could be talking about Saul and his group of followers or Absalom and his following– the context in which Psalm 14 was written is not known for sure. Either way the good people are being "eaten up" like bread by the wicked nonbelievers (vs. 4). In verse 7 David is looking forward to God rescuing his people and restoring their fortunes.

Fortunes could be actual wealth or spiritual fortune as people turn to God as their source.

Remember, though, when I told you that David speaks prophetically throughout the Psalms; this is one of those times. Besides the current need for salvation, David was

"Over a half century ago, while I was still a child, I recall hearing a number of old people offer the following explanation for the great disasters that had befallen <u>Russia</u>: 'Men have forgotten God; that's why all this has happened.' Since then, I have spent well-nigh 50 years working on the history of our revolution; in the process I have read hundreds of books, collected hundreds of personal testimonies, and have already contributed eight volumes of my own toward the effort of clearing away the rubble left by that upheaval. But if I were asked today to formulate as concisely as possible the main cause of the ruinous revolution that swallowed up some 60 million of our people, I could not put it more accurately than to repeat: 'Men have forgotten God; that's why all this has happened.'"

2. <u>Theodore Beale</u>: "…there have been twenty-eight countries in world history that can be confirmed to have been ruled by regimes with avowed atheists at the helm…These twenty-eight historical regimes have been ruled by eighty-nine atheists…The total body count for the ninety years between 1917 and 2007 is approximately 148 million dead at the bloody hands of fifty-two atheists, three times more than all the human beings killed by war, civil war, and individual crime in the entire twentieth century combined."

also speaking of mankind's need for salvation. Here he is prophesying of the Messiah who would come out of Zion (Jerusalem) to restore the Jews to their rightful place with God through Jesus' sacrifice on the cross (God sent Jesus first for the Jews and then the Gentiles- Romans 1:16).

Let's go a step further. Zion in its literal meaning is the physical Jerusalem on Earth, but it also represents the heavenly Jerusalem (God's kingdom in Heaven). Zion is also His kingdom on Earth, which is established through us (the church). If Zion represents us, then we are, according to verse 7, part of the salvation of Israel. We are to support Israel and pray for her (Genesis 12:3, Romans 15:27). We are also part of the salvation of the world in that we are to spread God's kingdom on Earth (Matthew 24:14). We are to share the truth of the gospel until the day God calls us to join Him in His heavenly kingdom.

Okay, this is a complex topic, one in which we have barely scratched the surface, and I have one more nugget for you. If you read Romans 11:25-27 you will see that David's prophecy goes even further to the second coming of Jesus when the heavenly Jerusalem will descend from Heaven and will be established on Earth in place of the current Jerusalem (Matthew 25:31-34, Revelation 21:1-5). Then all those who made God their refuge, who sought after Him and made Him their vital necessity, will eternally be restored to God. Then everyone will truly rejoice and be glad for all eternity (vs. 7)!

Prayer: God, I believe in you. You are my creator and my refuge. Evil is all around me and people have rejected you, but I stand with you. I pray right now for the spirit of truth to invade this world and open the hearts of mankind. Help them to see the truth of the gospel and be receptive as missionaries, preachers, and evangelists bring forth the truth.

I pray that atheists, Buddhists, Muslims, Hindus, Mormons, Jehovah's Witnesses… will turn to you and repent. Father, I also pray for the Jewish people to know Jesus as their Messiah. I pray for the protection of your people from those who wish to harm them. I bless Israel in Jesus' name and I am joyful knowing that you hear my prayer. I rejoice knowing that you will bring salvation and will restore the fortunes of your people. Amen.

Week 14 Day 1 Notes for Psalm 14: Which verse stood out to you the most and why?

_____

_____

_____

_____

What important life lesson can you apply from this Psalm?

_____

_____

_____

_____

_____

Week 14 Day 2 Devotions: Reread Psalm 14:1 and the following verses on not believing in God and corruption.

Ephesians 4:18 *for their [moral] understanding is darkened and their reasoning is clouded; [they are] alienated and self-banished from the life of God [with no share in it; this is] because of the [willful] ignorance and spiritual blindness that is [deep-seated] within them, because of the hardness and insensitivity of their heart.*

2 Timothy 3:1-5 *But understand this, that in the last days dangerous times [of great stress and trouble] will come [difficult days that will be hard to bear]. For people will be lovers of self [narcissistic, self-focused], lovers of money [impelled by greed], boastful, arrogant, revilers, disobedient to parents, ungrateful, unholy and profane, [and they will be] unloving [devoid of natural human affection, calloused and inhumane], irreconcilable, malicious gossips, devoid of self-control [intemperate, immoral], brutal, haters of good, traitors, reckless, conceited, lovers of [sensual] pleasure rather than lovers of God, holding to a form of [outward] godliness (religion), although they have denied its power [for their conduct nullifies their claim of faith]. Avoid such people and keep far away from them.*

Hosea 9:9 *They have deeply corrupted (perverted) themselves As in the days of Gibeah. The LORD will remember their wickedness and guilt; He will punish their sins.*

Based on Ephesians 4, why is a person's "moral understanding darkened?"

_____

_____

List 3 of the traits from 2 Timothy 3 that you feel are the worst and that you see more of in the world than you did 5-10 years ago.

_____

_____

We have been instructed to "avoid such people and keep far away from them." Yet, we know we are instructed to be witnesses for God and that these people will be "punished for their sins." We have to love them but not live like them, be friendly but not accept their sin. How can you personally be a witness without fraternizing (mingling as brothers) with corrupt people?

_____

_____

_____

Week 14 Day 3 Devotions: Reread Psalm 14:2-3 and the following examples of God not finding any good people on Earth – the flood, Tower of Babel, and Sodom and Gomorrah.

Genesis 7:1, 4-5 *Then the LORD said to Noah, "Come into the ark, you with all your household, for you [alone] I have seen as righteous (doing what is right) before Me in this generation. For in seven days I am going to cause it to rain on the earth for forty days and forty nights; and I will destroy (blot out, wipe away) every living thing that I have made from the surface of the earth." So Noah did all that the LORD commanded him.*

Genesis 11:4-6, 9 *They said, "Come, let us build a city for ourselves, and a tower whose top will reach into the heavens, and let us make a [famous] name for ourselves, so that we will not be scattered [into separate groups] and be dispersed over the surface of the entire earth [as the LORD instructed]." Now the LORD came down to see the city and the tower which the sons of men had built. And the LORD said, "Behold, they are one [unified] people, and they all have the same language. This is only the beginning of what they will do [in rebellion against Me], and now no evil thing they imagine they can do will be impossible for them. Therefore the name of the city was Babel—because there the LORD confused the language of the entire earth; and from that place the LORD scattered and dispersed them over the surface of all the earth.*

Genesis 18:20, 32 [20] *And the LORD said, "The outcry [of the sin] of Sodom and Gomorrah is indeed great, and their sin is exceedingly grave.* [32] *Then Abraham said, "Oh may the Lord not be angry [with me], and I will speak only this once; suppose ten [righteous people] are found there?" And He said, "I will not destroy it for the sake of the ten."* **Genesis 19: 17, 24-26** *When they had brought them outside, one [of the angels] said, "Escape for your life! Do not look behind you, or stop anywhere in the entire valley; escape to the mountains [of Moab], or you will* *be consumed and swept away."* [24] *Then the* LORD *rained down brimstone (flaming sulfur) and fire on Sodom and on Gomorrah from the* LORD *out of heaven,* [25] *and He overthrew (demolished, ended) those cities, and the entire valley, and all the inhabitants of the cities, and whatever grew on the ground.* [26] *But Lot's wife, from behind him, [foolishly, longingly] looked [back toward Sodom in an act of disobedience], and she became a pillar of salt.*

God searched for righteous people and right intentions in these verses before destroying or scattering them, and Abraham bargained with God for 10 verses in Genesis 18. What does this show you about God's nature?

_____

_____

_____

What reason did the people in Genesis 11 give for building the Tower of Babel?

_____

_____

_____

What does their reason for building and God's reason for scattering show you about the nature of people?

_____

_____

_____

If you read the entire story of Lot, you might ask yourself how in the world he was spared. He was nearly the same as his wife who "longingly looked back" at the city and was destroyed. What does her reaction show you about the nature of people?

_____

_____

_____

In what ways do you see these attitudes (natures) being exhibited in the world today? Write down one specific example for each of the responses you wrote.

_____

_____

_____

Week 14 Day 4 Devotions: Reread Psalm 14:4 and the following verses on not having knowledge, being ignorant.

Proverbs 1:7 *The [reverent] fear of the LORD [that is, worshiping Him and regarding Him as truly awesome] is the beginning and the preeminent part of knowledge [its starting point and its essence]; But arrogant fools despise [skillful and godly] wisdom and instruction and self-discipline.*

1 Peter 1:14-15 *[Live] as obedient children [of God]; do not be conformed to the evil desires which governed you in your ignorance [before you knew the requirements and transforming power of the good news regarding salvation]. But like the Holy One who called you, be holy yourselves in all your conduct [be set apart from the world by your godly character and moral courage];*

Acts 17:30 *Therefore God overlooked and disregarded the former ages of ignorance; but now He commands all people everywhere to repent [that is, to change their old way of thinking, to regret their past sins, and to seek God's purpose for their lives],*

People who "work iniquity" have no knowledge. What is the beginning of knowledge based on Proverbs 1?

_____

What did you used to do before you were called by God and came to the knowledge of salvation according to 1 Peter 1?

_____

God does not excuse ignorance but wants repentance. Define repentance in your own words based on Acts 17.

_____

_____

_____

If there is anything you need to repent for today, don't waste one more minute; give it to Him, change your thinking, and seek God's purpose for your life.

Week 14 Day 5 Devotions: Reread Psalm 14:5 and the following verses on the righteous trembling with fear of the Lord.

Proverbs 28:14 (NIV) *Blessed is the one who always trembles before God, but whoever hardens their heart falls into trouble.*

2 Corinthians 7:15 (NIV) *And his affection for you is all the greater when he remembers that you were all obedient, receiving him with fear and trembling.*

Philippians 2:12 *So then, my dear ones, just as you have always obeyed [my instructions with enthusiasm], not only in my presence, but now much more in my absence, continue to work out your salvation [that is, cultivate it, bring it to full effect, actively pursue spiritual maturity] with awe-inspired fear and trembling [using serious caution and critical self-evaluation to avoid anything that might offend God or discredit the name of Christ].*

Why should you "tremble before God?"

_____

_____

_____

According to Philippians 2, What does it mean to "work out your salvation?"

_____

_____

_____

How can you actively do this today?

_____

_____

_____

After reading these verses, what do you think it means to "fear and tremble" and is it different than what you have thought in the past?

_____

_____

_____

Week 14 Day 6 Devotions: Reread Psalm 14:6 and the following verses on the poor.

Isaiah 25:4 *For You have been a stronghold for the helpless, A stronghold for the poor in his distress, A shelter from the storm, a shade from the heat; For the breath of tyrants Is like a rainstorm against a wall.*

Proverbs 14:31 *He who oppresses the poor taunts and insults his Maker, But he who is kind and merciful and gracious to the needy honors Him.*

Deuteronomy 15:11 *For the poor will never cease to be in the land; therefore I command you, saying, 'You shall freely open your hand to your brother, to your needy, and to your poor in your land.'*

God is a _____ for the poor and helpless. People who

_____ the poor taunt and _____

God, while those who are _____ and merciful _____ Him.

In Deuteronomy 15 God commands you to _____

_____

Describe a specific way you can obey this commandment today?

_____

_____

Week 14 Day 7 Devotions: Reread Psalm 14:7 and the following verses about God restoring Israel.

Amos 9:14-15 (ESV) *I will restore the fortunes of my people Israel, and they shall rebuild the ruined cities and inhabit them; they shall plant vineyards and drink their wine, and they shall make gardens and eat their fruit. I will plant them on their land, and they shall never again be uprooted out of the land that I have given them," says the Lord your God.*

Isaiah 49:6 *He says, "It is too trivial a thing that You should be My Servant To raise up the tribes of Jacob and to restore the survivors of Israel; I will also make You a light to the nations That My salvation may reach to the end of the earth."*

Acts 3:20-21 *and that He may send [to you] Jesus, the Christ, who has been appointed for you, whom heaven must keep until the time for the [complete] restoration of all things about which God promised through the mouth of His holy prophets from ancient time.*

God's first priority is to restore His chosen people and bless them. They were declared a nation again on May 14, 1948. What does God promise for them in Amos 9?

_____

_____

_____

Why does God tell Isaiah that it is too trivial, small, a thing that he only be sent to the Jews?

_____

_____

_____

You have access now, through Jesus, to the same promise of restoration and blessings! What do you think about that?

_____

_____

_____

_____

Week 15 Day 1: Psalm 15

¹ Lord, who shall dwell [temporarily] in Your tabernacle? Who shall dwell [permanently] on Your holy hill?
² He who walks and lives uprightly and blamelessly, who works rightness and justice and speaks and thinks the truth in his heart,
³ He who does not slander with his tongue, nor does evil to his friend, nor takes up a reproach against his neighbor;
⁴ In whose eyes a vile person is despised, but he who honors those who fear the Lord (who revere and worship Him); who swears to his own hurt and does not change;
⁵ [He who] does not put out his money for [a]interest [to one of his own people] and who will not take a bribe against the innocent. He who does these things shall never be moved.

Side Note: bibleq.net

1. YHVH is used 6,807 times in the Bible followed by Elohim, which is used 2,340 times. Elohim means the Creator and Judge of the universe. It is also used in scripture to emphasize God's might.

Prayer: Holy God, Great Creator, you are mighty, and I stand in awe of you. I am so

"**LORD**, who will **dwell** in Your **tabernacle?**" (vs. 1) I would like to focus on three words from this verse for a few moments. I believe it will make the rest of chapter 15 more poignant if we can explore the meaning and significance of them. When we see the name LORD in capital letters it is the proper name for God. His name in Hebrew is spelled YHVH, which is pronounced Yod Hey Vav Hey in Hebrew. However, the Jewish tradition is to substitute Adonai, "my Lord," or Heshem, "the name," instead of pronouncing it because the name is so sacred. They did this out of reverence for God (Hebrew4Christians.com). YHVH in English is spelled Yahweh. In English, we use Yahweh interchangeably with Jehovah. His name means life giver, performer of His promises, the one who is, the absolute unchangeable one, the God of redemption, the one who will be with thee, and the everlasting one (Biblehub.com– Strong's Hebrew 3068).

The word dwell means to reside, inhabit, to live or continue in, or to establish one's self. The tabernacle was a mobile tent with special furniture that was erected as the Israelites traveled through the wilderness, as recounted in the book of Exodus. God gave very specific directions as to its construction. The tabernacle was the dwelling place of God's divine presence (Exodus 25:8-9, 29:45-46). Later the same word is used to describe Jesus in John 1:14 as He became flesh and made His dwelling among us. Dwelling in this verse is the same word as the Old Testament word that was used for tabernacle. God came in flesh to dwell or tabernacle among His people, so the word tabernacle represents the very real presence of God on Earth.

After Jesus was translated, the Holy Spirit was sent to dwell in those who believe that Jesus is the risen Messiah (Ephesians 1:13, Romans 8:9). This means that God's presence is in each Christian. We are now His tabernacle, His dwelling place, and He tabernacles, dwells, with us. This is a true picture of communion, fellowship, and companionship.

Before Jesus came and rent the veil, only the chosen priest could enter into God's holy presence and only on certain

blessed to be able to come to you and dwell with you. I am honored that you have chosen to dwell with me. I do not take this privilege lightly. I pray that through the power of the Holy Spirit at work in me I will never be the same sinful person again. I want to live a holy life that honors you. Change me into your image as I read the Word and spend time with you each day. Thank you, LORD for all that you have done in me and will continue to do until your return or my passing. Amen.

occasions. Now we can live, reside, and establish ourselves in God's presence through the Holy Spirit in us. This is significant because when David wrote Psalm 15, he was not allowed into the Holy of Holies in the tabernacle. He did experience the presence of God, but he longed to stay in God's presence as we will see later in the Psalms.

We need to grasp how special this privilege is that we have. Thinking back to the explanation of what the name of the LORD means, we should realize who we are dealing with. We should understand what it means to dwell in His presence and what an honor it is that He not only allows us this companionship but desires to commune with us. Now that we have established the background information for verse 1, let's look at it again: God Almighty, Holy God, Life-giver, Performer of Promises, and Everlasting One, who will reside, who will establish themselves and commune in Your presence?

The depth of David's question is profound. The rest of verse 1 is a continuation of the first question he asks. This time his question moves heavenward. Who will dwell in Heaven with You for eternity? Verses 2-5 give us the answer to his two questions. It is not enough to simply believe in Jesus and get our "get out of hell" card. God desires us to live holy lives that are set apart from the world. We must strive to be transformed, new creations (Romans 12:2, 2 Corinthians 5:16-18). What is expected of us? David says we are to live pure lives, and we are to do right, be just, speak truth, and think truth (vs. 2). We are not to badmouth people or treat people badly (vs. 3). We are to hate evil and disgusting things. We are to honor people who revere and worship God. We are to be people who keep their promises and are consistent (vs. 4). Finally, we are not to use our money against people or to hurt them- to take advantage of them (vs. 5).

David is basically saying that the people who follow verses 2-5 will be the ones dwelling in God's presence. David sets the bar high, but God knows we cannot reach it without His help. He knows that as long as we live in a fallen world, we will not achieve perfection. That is why he sent Jesus and why we must have the Holy Spirit living in us. God's unimaginable grace is not a license to sin as some think; on the contrary, Romans 6:14 says that we are now free from sin's control because of grace (also refer to Romans 8:1-15). While we may sin after we become Christians, we have God's grace and the power of the Holy Spirit to help us not to sin. While we will not reach perfection on this earth, we must strive to be holy because a holy God dwells in us and us in Him.

Week 15 Day 1 Notes for Psalm 15: Which verse stood out to you the most and why?

_____

_____

_____

_____

What important life lesson can you apply from this Psalm?

_____

_____

_____

_____

Week 15 Day 2 Devotions: Reread Psalm 15:1 and the following verses on dwelling with God.

Psalm 91:9-10 _Because you have made the LORD, [who is] my refuge, Even the Most High, your dwelling place,_ _10 No evil will befall you, Nor will any plague come near your tent._

Ephesians 2:22 _In Him [and in fellowship with one another] you also are being built together into a dwelling place of God in the Spirit._

Revelation 21:3 _and then I heard a loud voice from the throne, saying, "See! The tabernacle of God is among men, and He will live among them, and they will be His people, and God Himself will be with them as their God,]_

What does God say will happen if you make Him your dwelling place?

_____

_____

Where does God dwell according to Ephesians 2 and Revelations 21?

_____

_____

Week 15 Day 3 Devotions: Reread Psalm 15:2 and the following verses on integrity.

Proverbs 11:3 _The integrity and moral courage of the upright will guide them, But the crookedness of the treacherous will destroy them._

Proverbs 10:9 *He who walks in integrity and with moral character walks securely, but he who takes a crooked way will be discovered and punished.*

Proverbs 2:7 *He stores away sound wisdom for the righteous [those who are in right standing with Him]; He is a shield to those who walk in integrity [those of honorable character and moral courage],*

At some point in the school year I will write the word "integrity" on the board and tell my students, "Because I try to have integrity." This is a response to some kind of, "Why can't we do…" question, "No one will know if…" or "The other teachers…" Though I mess up every single day, I try to live with integrity so I can have a positive testimony for my students and fellow teachers. It's those small things that you don't compromise that will shine His light for others to see.

According to Proverbs, integrity will guide you, make you secure, and protect you. In what little or big things can you show integrity today (be specific)?

_____

_____

Week 15 Day 4 Devotions: Reread Psalm 15:3 and the following verses on lying.

Proverbs 6:16-19 *These six things the LORD hates; Indeed, seven are repulsive to Him: A proud look [the attitude that makes one overestimate oneself and discount others], a lying tongue, And hands that shed innocent blood, A heart that creates wicked plans, Feet that run swiftly to evil, A false witness who breathes out lies [even half-truths], And one who spreads discord (rumors) among brothers.*

Exodus 20:16 *"You shall not testify falsely [that is, lie, withhold, or manipulate the truth] against your neighbor (any person).*

Revelation 21:8 *But as for the cowards and unbelieving and abominable [who are devoid of character and personal integrity and practice or tolerate immorality], and murderers, and sorcerers [with intoxicating drugs], and idolaters and occultists [who practice and teach false religions], and all the liars [who knowingly deceive and twist truth], their part will be in the lake that blazes with fire and brimstone, which is the second death."*

What 3 things does God hate that involve the mouth in Proverbs 6?

_____

_____

What is the definition of lying based on Exodus 20 and Revelations 21?

_____

_____

We are all guilty of twisting the truth or leaving bits of truth out of a story or excuse. Ask the Holy Spirit to guard your mouth today and speak His truth to you and through you.

Week 15 Day 5 Devotions: Reread Psalm 15:4 and the following verses on God honoring people who obey Him and punishing those who do not honor Him.

1 Samuel 2:30 *Therefore the LORD God of Israel declares, 'I did indeed say that your house and that of [Aaron] your father would walk [in priestly service] before Me forever.' But now the LORD declares, 'Far be it from Me—for those who honor Me I will honor, and those who despise Me will be insignificant and contemptible.*

Deuteronomy 7:9-10 *Therefore know [without any doubt] and understand that the LORD your God, He is God, the faithful God, who is keeping His covenant and His [steadfast] lovingkindness to a thousand generations with those who love Him and keep His commandments; but repays those who hate Him to their faces, by destroying them; He will not hesitate with him who hates Him, He will repay him to his face.*

Deuteronomy 7:12-13 *"Then it shall come about, because you listen to these judgments and keep and do them, that the LORD your God will keep with you the covenant and the [steadfast] lovingkindness which He swore to your fathers. He will love you and bless you and multiply you; He will also bless the fruit of your womb and the fruit of your land, your grain and your new wine and your [olive] oil, the offspring of your cattle and the young of your flock, in the land which He swore to your fathers to give you.*

What are the conditions to the promises listed in these verses?

_____

_____

Looking at theses 3 verses, how is it worth it to you to honor God in obedience today?

_____

_____

_____

_____

Week 15 Day 6 Devotions: Reread Psalm 15:4 and the following verses on God keeping His word.

Psalm 89:33-35 *"Nevertheless, I will not break off My lovingkindness from him, Nor allow My faithfulness to fail. "My covenant I will not violate, Nor will I alter the utterance of My lips. "Once [for all] I have sworn by My holiness, [My vow which cannot be violated]; I will not lie to David.*

Numbers 23:19 *"God is not a man, that He should lie, Nor a son of man, that He should repent. Has He said, and will He not do it? Or has He spoken and will He not make it good and fulfill it?*

Deuteronomy 7:9 *Therefore know [without any doubt] and understand that the LORD your God, He is God, the faithful God, who is keeping His covenant and His [steadfast] lovingkindness to a thousand generations with those who love Him and keep His commandments;*

God swears by His _____, not ours. This means you can know

"[_____]" that He will be _____

and keep His word.

Briefly describe 1 instance where God has kept His word to you.

_____

_____

_____

Week 15 Day 7 Devotions: Reread Psalm 15:5 interest and the following verses on charging interest and taking bribes.

Proverbs 21:14 *A gift in secret subdues anger, and a bribe [hidden] in the pocket, strong wrath.*

2 Chronicles 19:7 *So now let the fear (reverent awe) of the LORD be on you [to keep you from making unjust decisions]; be careful in what you do, for there is no injustice with the LORD our God, or partiality, or acceptance of a bribe."*

Leviticus 25:35-37 *'Now if your fellow countryman becomes poor and his hand falters with you [that is, he has trouble repaying you for something], then you are to help and sustain him, [with courtesy and consideration] like [you would] a stranger or a temporary resident [without property], so that he may live among you. Do not charge him usurious interest, but fear your God [with profound reverence], so your countryman may [continue to] live among you. ³⁷ You shall not give him your money at interest, nor your food at a profit.*

Money is mentioned over 800 times in the Bible. Why do you think God is so concerned about using money wisely and being honest with your money?

_____

_____

_____

How do you see people misusing money or being dishonest with it in the world today?

_____

_____

_____

_____

What can you personally do to make sure you use money correctly today (be specific)?

_____

_____

_____

_____

Week 16 Day 1: Psalm 16

¹ Keep and protect me, O God, for in You I have found refuge, and in You do I put my trust and hide myself.
² I say to the Lord, You are my Lord; I have no good beside or beyond You.
³ As for the godly (the saints) who are in the land, they are the excellent, the noble, and the glorious, in whom is all my delight.
⁴ Their sorrows shall be multiplied who choose another god; their drink offerings of blood will I not offer or take their names upon my lips.
⁵ The Lord is my chosen and assigned portion, my cup; You hold and maintain my lot.
⁶ The lines have fallen for me in pleasant places; yes, I have a good heritage.
⁷ I will bless the Lord, Who has given me counsel; yes, my heart instructs me in the night seasons.
⁸ I have set the Lord continually before me; because He is at my right hand, I shall not be moved.
⁹ Therefore my heart is glad and my glory [my inner self] rejoices; my body too shall rest and confidently dwell in safety,
¹⁰ For You will not abandon me to Sheol (the place of the dead), neither will You suffer Your holy one [Holy One] to see corruption.

David fled the city with 300 men, while Saul followed him with 3000 soldiers. They were closing in, and David was nearly surrounded when news of a Philistine invasion reached King Saul. He and his men were forced to turn back, and thus David's life was spared once more. This is most likely when David penned Psalm 16. The first thing I thought of after reading Psalm 16 and researching the context in which it was written was how God spared David's life over and over again. This showed me several things:

1. God allows trials into our lives to develop our character, burn off excess junk, and prepare us for our future. I mean David was the future king and a man after God's own heart, but he was hated and hunted many times during his life. If he went through storms, why would we expect to be any different? **2.** David, though fearful and depressed at times, ultimately stood firm in God as his source and salvation. David could have cursed God because of the injustice and evil he saw the world, but he didn't. Instead, he rested in God's sovereignty and goodness, and we should too. **3.** What God anoints or ordains He will protect. Nothing but our own choices can detour God's plans for our life, and His plans for us are good (Jeremiah 29:11). Though the enemy surrounds us on every side, we will not be overcome (1 John 4:4). He will fight for us, protect us, and bless us as we trust and obey Him.

David trusted in God to the fullest extent and hid himself under the presence of God during troubled times (vs. 1) He took refuge in God's promises and in his knowledge that God is a promise keeper. David understood that every good thing in his life came from God, and that God was the best thing in his life (vs. 2).

In verses 3 and 4 David compares the godly to the unbeliever. The godly are excellent (exemplary and outstanding), noble (honorable and admirable), and glorious (delightful and magnificent), and it pleased David's heart to see them. In contrast, those who rejected God and served other gods were full of sorrow (distress, grief, and regret). Pagan religions often called for blood sacrifices, many of

11 You will show me the path of life; in Your presence is fullness of joy, at Your right hand there are pleasures forevermore.

Side Note:

jewishvirtuallibrary.org

1. Christianity 2.1 billion
2. Islam 31.6 billion
3. Agnostic 1.1 billion
4. Hinduism 1 billion
5. Chinese Folk Religion 394 million
6. Buddhism 376 million
7. Tribal Religions 300 million
8. Sikhism 23 million
9. Judaism 14 million
10. Jainism 4.2 million
11. Shintoism 4 million
12. nitarian-Universalism 800,000
13. Rastafarianism 600,000
14. Scientology 500,000

Prayer: I set you always before me, God, as a priority in my life. Because I have you by my side I will not be moved! Because of this, I am glad and hopeful. I rest in you because you will not allow me to be shaken or overtaken by the world or the enemy. Even death cannot harm me for I have eternal life in you. I will live in your presence and have joy and blessings from you on Earth and for all eternity. Hallelujah! Amen!

which were human. Think of the sorrow the families of those human sacrifices experienced as a loved one was lost forever, and their sorrows were multiplied because the bloodshed was for naught. The false gods could not answer their prayers or save them, so they lived and died without help, hope, or the promise of Heaven.

What sorrow it is to know that 2.9 billion people around the world still live like this today (see side note and sacredoutfitter.blogspot.com). Generation after generation they are born into the sorrow of a world without a Savior, but David has the answer; he has chosen God! God is the holder of all David has, all David is, and all he will be (vs. 5). God has provided David with a good inheritance, and he is pleased and content with it (vs. 6). He will bless (honor, glorify, and exalt) God who has guided his life, given him wisdom, and even taught him well in the night seasons (vs. 7). Night seasons could literally mean that God instructed David while he was sleeping (Job 33:15, Matthew 2:12 and 27:19), but he could also be referring to the dark storms he faced in his life while being hunted by Saul and Absalom. Either way God has promised to teach us, give us wisdom, and speak to us through the Holy Spirit.

The next 4 verses switch gears a bit and have a triple meaning. The first meaning is a literal one where David is speaking about himself. David put God first in his life and put God in authority over his life (at his right hand vs. 8). God had power and dominion over David because he willingly submitted to Him. Because David did this, he knows he is safe and stable. No one can move him out of God's hand or change God's will for his life (vs. 8). Because of this revelation, David's heart is glad, and he rejoices. His body and emotions are at peace, and he rests confidently in God (vs. 9).

David has a calling on his life that must be fulfilled, so he knows that God is protecting him on Earth. He also has the hope of Heaven after he dies. God will not ever abandon him (vs. 10)! David trusts God to show him where to go and how to get there. He is confident that God's way will lead him to full life and into life eternal (vs.11). In this life journey of abiding in God's presence, David will have joy and pleasure. However, he will have the fullness of everything God is and everything God has for him when he reaches Heaven.

The second meaning of these 4 verses is prophetic. David paints a picture of our Savior after He has risen from the dead and is seated at God's right hand. In Ephesians 1:19-21, Paul tells us that Jesus is seated at God's right hand and has authority over all things. Peter even uses Psalm 16:8-11 in Acts 2:25-28 as he explains to the astonished crowd of onlookers the life, death, and resurrection of Jesus. He says that David foretold the resurrection of Jesus in Psalm 16, and that Jesus is the fulfillment of that prophecy. The Holy Spirit revealed this knowledge to Peter and empowered his speech so that the message "stung (cut) to the heart," and over 3000 souls were added to the kingdom of God that day!

The joy expressed by David and recounted by Peter 2,000 years later is the polar opposite of the sorrow felt by those who follow false gods. As their grief and heartache is multiplied because of not choosing to follow the one true God, so the joy and pleasure multiplies for the believer because of what Jesus did on the cross. When Peter retells David's revelation he says, "My flesh will encamp, pitch its tent, and dwell in hope" in the knowledge of Jesus' resurrection, and that God "enraptures me defusing my soul with joy with and in your presence." This is why Psalm 16 is titled Miktam or Michtam. It is one of 6 titled in this manner. It is believed to mean golden, implying something to be treasured because it is precious. It also stems from a Hebrew word meaning an engraving. Others believe it is related to a word meaning "to hide," thus signifying a secret. When putting all this together, along with the fulfilled prophetic meaning of the Psalm itself, Psalm 16 could be titled "The Psalm of the Precious Secret." (Treasury of David-Spurgeon.org)

The cherished knowledge of the Gospel and hope we have for eternal life was a secret told to David over 2,000 years before its fulfillment. It was worthy of engraving on stone for its preservation. Now it is worthy of engraving on our hearts as we accept Jesus as our Lord and Savior.

Finally, the third meaning is a personal declaration and confession. I graduated from a Christian high school and was asked to give a devotion at our Senior Tea. I had never had to do something like that before, so I prayed about what to say. God led me to Psalm 16 and focused me on verses 8-11. This passage of scripture became my set of life verses and becomes the prayer for this Psalm.

Week 16 Day 1 Notes for Psalm 16: Which verse stood out to you the most and why?

_____

_____

_____

_____

What important life lesson can you apply from this Psalm?

_____

_____

_____

_____

Week 16 Day 2 Devotions: Reread Psalm 16:1-2 and the following verses on having nothing good without God.

John 15:4-5 *Remain in Me, and I [will remain] in you. Just as no branch can bear fruit by itself without remaining in the vine, neither can you [bear fruit, producing evidence of your faith] unless you remain in Me. I am the Vine; you are the branches. The one who remains in Me and I in him bears much fruit, for [otherwise] apart from Me [that is, cut off from vital union with Me] you can do nothing.*

James 1:17 *Every good thing given and every perfect gift is from above; it comes down from the Father of lights [the Creator and Sustainer of the heavens], in whom there is no variation [no rising or setting] or shadow cast by His turning [for He is perfect and never changes].*

Philippians 2:13 *For it is [not your strength, but it is] God who is effectively at work in you, both to will and to work [that is, strengthening, energizing, and creating in you the longing and the ability to fulfill your purpose] for His good pleasure.*

What does John 15 tell you the benefits of remaining in God have for your life?

_____

_____

According to Philippians 2, what good things come from God?

_____

_____

Knowing that every good thing you have ever received comes from God should cause you to be thankful. List as many good things as you can that you have received from Him.

_____

_____

_____

_____

Week 16 Day 3 Devotions: Reread Psalm 16:4 and the following verses on serving other gods.

Exodus 20:3-4 *"You shall have no other gods before Me. ⁴ "You shall not make for yourself any idol, or any likeness (form, manifestation) of what is in heaven above or on the earth beneath or in the water under the earth [as an object to worship].*

Matthew 6:24 *"No one can serve two masters; for either he will hate the one and love the other, or he will be devoted to the one and despise the other. You cannot serve God and mammon [money, possessions, fame, status, or whatever is valued more than the Lord].*

Philippians 3:18-19 *For there are many, of whom I have often told you, and now tell you even with tears, who live as enemies of the cross of Christ [rejecting and opposing His way of salvation], whose fate is destruction, whose god is their belly [their worldly appetite, their sensuality, their vanity], and whose glory is in their shame—who focus their mind on earthly and temporal things.*

List what other gods/idols are based on these verses.

_____

_____

_____

_____

_____

Have you ever put anything in front of God as a priority in your life, whether listed in these verses or not? Write what it *was* or *is* down.

_____

_____

_____

_____

How did you put your priorities in the correct order (share what you've learned and accomplished with someone) OR how can you reprioritize today?

_____

_____

_____

_____

Week 16 Day 4 Devotions: Reread Psalm 16:5-6 and the following verses on our inheritance from God as His children.

Galatians 4:4-7 *But when [in God's plan] the proper time had fully come, God sent His Son, born of a woman, born under the [regulations of the] Law, so that He might redeem and liberate those who were under the Law, that we [who believe] might be adopted as sons [as God's children with all rights as fully grown members of a family]. And because you [really] are [His] sons, God has sent the Spirit of His Son into our hearts, crying out, "Abba! Father!" Therefore you are no longer a slave (bond-servant), but a son; and if a son, then also an heir through [the gracious act of] God [through Christ].*

Romans 8:17 *And if [we are His] children, [then we are His] heirs also: heirs of God and fellow heirs with Christ [sharing His spiritual blessing and inheritance], if indeed we share in His suffering so that we may also share in His glory.*

Ephesians 3:6 *[it is this:] that the Gentiles are now joint heirs [with the Jews] and members of the same body, and joint partakers [sharing] in the [same divine] promise in Christ Jesus through [their faith in] the good news [of salvation].*

According to Galatians 4, you have been _____ by God and thus

have as His children _____ rights. You can call God your _____!

You are no longer a _____, but a _____ and an

_____ through Christ.

What do you share with Christ according to Romans 8?

_____

_____

Even though suffering is one thing we may share with Jesus, we have salvation and glory as a promise. Talk to God as your Heavenly Father today. No matter what kind of earthly father you have, don't judge God by him. Get in the Word and learn who God is and who you are to Him. It will change you.

Week 16 Day 5 Devotion: Reread Psalm 16:8-9 and the following verses on keeping God as your focus.

Hebrews 12:2 *[looking away from all that will distract us and] focusing our eyes on Jesus, who is the Author and Perfecter of faith [the first incentive for our belief and the One who brings our faith to maturity], who for the joy [of accomplishing the goal] set before Him endured the cross, disregarding the shame, and sat down at the right hand of the throne of God [revealing His deity, His authority, and the completion of His work].*

Hebrews 3:1 (NIV) *Therefore, holy brothers and sisters, who share in the heavenly calling, fix your thoughts on Jesus, whom we acknowledge as our apostle and high priest.*

2 Corinthians 4:18 *So we look not at the things which are seen, but at the things which are unseen; for the things which are visible are temporal [just brief and fleeting], but the things which are invisible are everlasting and imperishable.*

What benefits do you have by keeping your focus on God?

_____

_____

_____

_____

In what specific ways can you keep you focus on God throughout the day?

_____

_____

_____

Week 16 Day 6 Devotions: Reread Psalm 16:10 and the following verses on eternal life.

John 3:16 *"For God so [greatly] loved and dearly prized the world, that He [even] gave His [One and] only begotten Son, so that whoever believes and trusts in Him [as Savior] shall not perish, but have eternal life.*

1 John 5:13 *These things I have written to you who believe in the name of the Son of God [which represents all that Jesus Christ is and does], so that you will know [with settled and absolute knowledge] that you [already] have eternal life.*

John 10:28-30 *And I give them eternal life, and they will never, ever [by any means] perish; and no one will ever snatch them out of My hand. My Father, who has given them to Me, is greater and mightier than all; and no one is able to snatch them out of the Father's hand. I and the Father are One [in essence and nature]."*

What does Jesus' name represent? _____

Looking at 1 John 5, when you believe in His name what will you know and how will you know it?

_____

_____

What 2 assurances does John 10 give you?

_____

_____

Week 16 Day 7 Devotions: Reread Psalm 16:11 and the following verses on paths.

Proverbs 3:6 *In all your ways know and acknowledge and recognize Him, And He will make your paths straight and smooth [removing obstacles that block your way].*

Proverbs 4:26-27 *Consider well and watch carefully the path of your feet, And all your ways will be steadfast and sure. Do not turn away to the right nor to the left [where evil may lurk]; Turn your foot from [the path of] evil.*

Isaiah 26:7 *The way of the righteous [those in right-standing with God—living in moral and spiritual integrity] is smooth and level; O Upright One, make a level path for the just and righteous.*

What do you have to do to have straight paths based on these verses?

_____

_____

_____

_____

How can you "consider well and watch carefully" your path today (be specific)?

_____

_____

_____

_____

Week 17 Day 1: Psalm 17

¹ Hear the right (my righteous cause), O Lord; listen to my shrill, piercing cry! Give ear to my prayer, that comes from unfeigned and guileless lips.
² Let my sentence of vindication come from You! May Your eyes behold the things that are just and upright.
³ You have proved my heart; You have visited me in the night; You have tried me and find nothing [no evil purpose in me]; I have purposed that my mouth shall not transgress.
⁴ Concerning the works of men, by the word of Your lips I have avoided the ways of the violent (the paths of the destroyer).
⁵ My steps have held closely to Your paths [to the tracks of the One Who has gone on before]; my feet have not slipped.
⁶ I have called upon You, O God, for You will hear me; incline Your ear to me and hear my speech.
⁷ Show Your marvelous loving-kindness, O You Who save by Your right hand those who trust and take refuge in You from those who rise up against them.
⁸ Keep and guard me as the pupil of Your eye; hide me in the shadow of Your wings
⁹ From the wicked who despoil and oppress me, my deadly adversaries who surround me.

"... listen to my shrill, piercing cry!" (vs. 1) David is distressed, but not depressed, crushed but not abandoned, pressed in on every side but not destroyed (2 Corinthians 4:8). His prayer to God in Psalm 17 is strong and loud. He is screaming it out of a desperate need to be rescued, but he is confident that God will answer him because he is guiltless (vs. 1). He tells God to be his judge because God is just and upright (vs. 2). He knows God will vindicate him because God has searched David's heart, tested him, and found no evil purpose in him (vs. 3).

David has consciously decided to watch his mouth that he not lie or sin with it because that would go against God's Word (vs. 3). He will not follow the world's path that destroys others and would ultimately destroy him (vs. 4) but has chosen to follow the straight and narrow path consistently (vs. 5). David has chosen to call out to God because he knows God will hear him and show him how marvelous His love is (vs. 6, 7). When those in right standing with God are oppressed by people who would attack them physically or with words, God's right hand (mighty hand) will save them and protect them just like he protected David (vs. 7).

David tells us that God will keep and guard us as the pupil of His eye and hide us under His wings (vs. 8). Our sight is very precious to us. The eyes are protected by bone and eyelids, and we are often warned about guarding our eyes when playing as children, while out in the sun, or laboring with power tools. How often we have heard, "Be careful with that thing or you'll poke your eye out!" David is telling us here that God guards us like He would guard His own eye. This phrase is "an emblem of that which is tenderest and dearest, and therefore guarded with the most jealous care." (Biblehub.com) It gives us the sense that when someone hurts us, they are also hurting God. The second phrase in verse 8 shows God's parental nature toward us-His great care for His people. He spreads His mighty, all-encompassing arms around us so that nothing can harm us. By doing this, He is saying, "You'll have to come through me first!"

10 They are enclosed in their own prosperity and have shut up their hearts to pity; with their mouths they make exorbitant claims and proudly and arrogantly speak.
11 They track us down in each step we take; now they surround us; they set their eyes to cast us to the ground,
12 Like a lion greedy and eager to tear his prey, and as a young lion lurking in hidden places.
13 Arise, O Lord! Confront and forestall them, cast them down! Deliver my life from the wicked by Your sword,
14 From men by Your hand, O Lord, from men of this world [these poor moths of the night] whose portion in life is idle and vain. Their bellies are filled with Your hidden treasure [what You have stored up]; their children are satiated, and they leave the rest [of their] wealth to their babes.
15 As for me, I will continue beholding Your face in righteousness (rightness, justice, and right standing with You); I shall be fully satisfied, when I awake [to find myself] beholding Your form [and having sweet communion with You].

Side Note: innocenceproject. org, foxnews.com, and opendoorsuk.org

1. "...the few studies that have been done estimate that between 2.3% and 5% of

David tells us in verses 9-12 that wicked people will use their mouth to hurt godly people and seek to destroy them like a hungry lion tearing into its prey. Look at what David said next in verse 13. He charged God to arise and take swift, permanent action on his behalf. Moses did the same thing in Numbers 10:35. They were calling on God to come on the scene with power and to do whatever needed to be done. It was an acknowledgement that they could not control the situation, but they knew God could.

As God took care of David's enemies and delivered him, David continued to seek God's face (vs. 15). Look at what happens as a result of David's decision; he is completely satisfied in God's presence – not in the wealth that fattened the men of the world in verse 14. No, David is filled with visions of his holy, loving Father.

This Psalm was especially meaningful to me during the darkness of the storm I have shared with you previously. Our family faced a situation where a false accusation jeopardized someone's future. This person maintained their guiltlessness just as David did, but the words were enough to hurt them and tear us up inside. We were attacked and felt like we had been thrown to the wolves. We prayed a lot and God showed us, through the Holy Spirit, that what had happened was unjust and to support this person. I dove into the Psalms for comfort and wisdom. Verses 1-3 represented this person's desperate plea to God for justice. Verses 9-12 represented those who set themselves up against us, and verses 6-8 and 13 were our prayer to God on this person's behalf.

God brought us through the hurricane, but it was important for us to see vindication. We continued to fervently pray that this person's name would be cleared even though the situation was over. God spoke to my husband and told him that this person's name was cleared in His book and that His book was the most important one. God had already done verse 3 even though we had not seen it in the natural realm. We have not yet seen the final fulfillment of our prayers in the natural, but we are

all prisoners in the U.S. are innocent (for context, if just 1% of all prisoners are innocent, that would mean that more than 20,000 innocent people are in prison)."

2. Saeed Abedini had been beaten and tortured in the Iranian prison where he was to be held for the next 8 yrs. for being a Christian leader... Amen, he has since been released since writing this part of our study, but thousands more are held in prison in various countries around the world. "North Korea is the most dangerous place in the world to be a Christian for the 14th year in a row. Christians face arrest, torture, imprisonment and death for daring to believe there is a higher authority than the nation's leader, Kim Jong-un. Many follow Jesus in secret; parents often don't even tell their children about their faith for fear they will be revealed. Thousands of other Christians are trapped in horrific labour camps and isolated closed villages..."

keeping our eyes on Him (vs. 15). This is what will truly keep us satisfied.

Going through this situation opened my eyes to injustices all around me that I had not noticed before. It helped me to be very conscious about making premature judgments or making judgments without all of the facts. It also made my heart soften toward injustice around the world. I began paying attention to it on the news and to pray for people who were oppressed. Hundreds of thousands of innocent people are being kicked out of their homes and their countries by terrorists. I could empathize with the pastor who had been held in Iran for several years and really began to pray for God's justice in the world- not just for our situation (see side note).

Sometimes things come into our lives to open our eyes to a world that we didn't know existed- a world that needs spiritual warriors to get involved and to pray. If you or someone you know is facing an injustice and they are innocent, please share Psalm 17 with them. God knows their heart; He knows the truth. Call on Him to arise and act on their behalf because of His marvelous loving-kindness.

Prayer: Heavenly Father I come to you because I know you are just and righteous and I know you hear me. I ask you that your justice will take place in my life and the lives of people all across the world that are facing injustice. Those who are falsely accused, who are fleeing their country for fear that they will be killed, those who are being persecuted for being Christians and for worshiping you... I pray that your mighty hand will protect them. I pray that the wicked people who are attacking the innocent will get saved will turn their hearts over to you or else find judgment in your hands. Thank you for guarding me so carefully and lovingly under your wings. I will continue to seek your face and commune with you because this is what truly satisfies my soul. Amen.

Week 17 Day 1 Notes for Psalm 17: Which verse stood out to you the most and why?

_____

_____

_____

_____

What important life lesson can you apply from this Psalm?

_____

_____

_____

_____

_____

Week 17 Day 2 Devotions: Reread Psalm 17:1-2 and the following verses on justice and vindication.

Psalm 135:14 (NIV) _For the LORD will vindicate his people and have compassion on his servants._

<u>**Isaiah 63:1**</u> _[God's Vengeance on the Nations] Who is this who comes from Edom, with crimson-stained garments from Bozrah [in Edom], This One (the Messiah) who is majestic in His apparel, Marching in the greatness of His might? "It is I, [the One] who speaks in righteousness [proclaiming **vindication**], mighty to save."_

<u>**Proverbs 21:15**</u> _When **justice** is done, it is a joy to the righteous (the upright, the one in right standing with God), But to the evildoers it is disaster._

List 3 injustices you see in the world around you, even if they do not directly affect you.

_____

_____

_____

_____

_____

Ultimate justice and vindication come from God. We may see some form of justice and vindication on Earth in our lifetime. However, if we do not, it is guaranteed to come when God judges mankind at the end of the ages. Make sure to rejoice when you see justice and pray about injustices you see in your own life and in situations around you. Trust God to work in those situations.

Week 17 Day 3 Devotion: Reread Psalm 17:3-4 and the following verses on purity.

Matthew 5:8 *"Blessed [anticipating God's presence, spiritually mature] are the pure in heart [those with integrity, moral courage, and godly character], for they will see God.*

Psalm 119:9 *How can a young man keep his way pure? By keeping watch [on himself] according to Your word [conforming his life to Your precepts].*

1 Timothy 4:12 *Let no one look down on [you because of] your youth, but be an example and set a pattern for the believers in speech, in conduct, in love, in faith, and in [moral] purity.*

What does purity mean according to Matthew 5?

_____

_____

Based on Psalm 119, how can you stay pure today?

_____

_____

What kind of example are you supposed to set for others according to 1 Timothy 4?

_____

_____

Week 17 Day 4 Devotions: Reread Psalm 17:5 and the following verses in walking the straight and narrow path/following God's path.

Proverbs 2:20 *So you will walk in the way of good men [that is, those of personal integrity, moral courage and honorable character], And keep to the paths of the righteous.*

Isaiah 26:7 *The way of the righteous [those in right-standing with God—living in moral and spiritual integrity] is smooth and level; O Upright One, make a level path for the just and righteous.*

Jeremiah 6:16 *Thus says the LORD, "Stand by the roads and look; ask for the ancient paths, Where the good way is; then walk in it, And you will find rest for your souls. But they said, 'We will not walk in it!'*

What does Isaiah 26 say God will do for you as you walk "the way of the righteous?"

_____

_____

According to Jeremiah 6, what will happen to you when you walk the "ancient paths, where the good way is?"

_____

Why do you think some people refuse to walk this path even though they have these promises (if you personally have chosen in the past not to follow God's path for your life, write down why you refused)?

_____

_____

_____

_____

What encouragement can you give someone today to follow after God?

_____

_____

_____

_____

Week 17 Day 5 Devotions: Reread Psalm 17:7-8 and the following verses about being the apple of God's eye.

Zechariah 2:8 _For thus says the LORD of hosts, "After glory He has sent Me against the nations which plunder you—for he who touches you, touches the apple of His eye._

Deuteronomy 32:10-11 _"He found him in a desert land, In the howling wasteland of a wilderness; He kept circling him, He took care of him, He protected him as the apple of His eye. "As an eagle that protects its nest, That flutters over its young, He spread out His wings and took them, He carried them on His pinions._

Proverbs 7:2 _Keep my commandments and live, And keep my teaching and law as the apple of your eye._

What does Zechariah 2 teach you about God's response to those who oppose Israel?

_____

_____

_____

_____

_____

According to Deuteronomy 32, what does God do to the apple of His eye, which is 1ˢᵗ Israel and then you as His adopted child?

_____

_____

_____

_____

In Proverbs 7, we see that we are to keep God's law as the apple of our eye. Write down how you can do this using the actions you wrote down from Deuteronomy 32.

_____

_____

_____

_____

Week 17 Day 6 Devotions: Reread Psalm 17:11-12 and the following verses on lions lurking and attacking prey.

Daniel 6:22 *My God has sent His angel and has shut the mouths of the lions so that they have not hurt me, because I was found innocent before Him; and also before you, O king, I have committed no crime."*

2 Timothy 4:15-19 *Be on guard against him yourself, because he vigorously opposed our message. At my first trial no one supported me [as an advocate] or stood with me, but they all deserted me. May it not be counted against them [by God]. But the Lord stood by me and strengthened and empowered me, so that through me the [gospel] message might be fully proclaimed, and that all the Gentiles might hear it; and I was rescued from the mouth of the lion. The Lord will rescue me from every evil assault, and He will bring me safely into His heavenly kingdom; to Him be the glory forever and ever. Amen.*

Psalm 57:4 *My life is among lions; I must lie among those who breathe out fire—The sons of men whose teeth are spears and arrows, And their tongue a sharp sword.*

Sometimes we are physically attacked by the enemy, the lion, as in Daniel's case. However, many times the lion we face is figurative as in Paul's case of an unjust trial where no one supported him.

What does Paul tell us God did for him?

_____

_____

_____

This is true for you as well, but heed his advice in verse 15. Be on _____

What was David's "lion" in Psalm 57? _____

What lions have you faced or are facing right now? Trust God to rescue you.

_____

_____

_____

_____

Week 17 Day 7 Devotions: Reread Psalm 17:14-15 and the following verses on money and building earthly and not heavenly treasures.

Ecclesiastes 5:10 *He who loves money will not be satisfied with money, nor he who loves abundance with its gain. This too is vanity (emptiness).*

Revelation 3:17 *Because you say, "I am rich, and have prospered and grown wealthy, and have need of nothing," and you do not know that you are wretched and miserable and poor and blind and naked [without hope and in great need],*

Matthew 6:19-20 *"Do not store up for yourselves [material] treasures on earth, where moth and rust destroy, and where thieves break in and steal. But store up for yourselves treasures in heaven, where neither moth nor rust destroys, and where thieves do not break in and steal;*

What is the result of loving money according to Ecclesiastes 5 and Revelations 3?

_____

_____

_____

_____

What happens to earthly treasures?

_____

_____

_____

_____

What earthly treasures have you been working hard to get?

_____

_____

_____

_____

What heavenly treasures have you been working toward or can start working for today?

_____

_____

_____

_____

Week 18 Day 1: Psalm 18

1 I love You fervently and devotedly, O Lord, my Strength.
2 The Lord is my Rock, my Fortress, and my Deliverer; my God, my keen and firm Strength in Whom I will trust and take refuge, my Shield, and the Horn of my salvation, my High Tower.
3 I will call upon the Lord, Who is to be praised; so shall I be saved from my enemies.
4 The cords or bands of death surrounded me, and the streams of ungodliness and the torrents of ruin terrified me.
5 The cords of Sheol (the place of the dead) surrounded me; the snares of death confronted and came upon me.
6 In my distress [when seemingly closed in] I called upon the Lord and cried to my God; He heard my voice out of His temple (heavenly dwelling place), and my cry came before Him, into His [very] ears.
7 Then the earth quaked and rocked, the foundations also of the mountains trembled; they moved and were shaken because He was indignant and angry.
8 There went up smoke from His nostrils; and lightning out of His mouth devoured; coals were kindled by it.
9 He bowed the heavens also and came down; and thick darkness was under His feet.

This is the longest Psalm we have read so far, and there is so much David has to say and so much for us to learn. I decided to break Psalm 18 down into categories instead of going through it linearly, but I will make sure to note each verse as we cover it. First, we will look at David's character and then his actions in the Psalm. After that, we will look at God's character and His actions in regard to David and his enemies.

1. David fervently loved God and was devoted to Him completely (vs. 1). Fervent means that David loved God with intensity, fire, and passion. This was no halfhearted or shallow emotion.
2. David pleased God and he delighted (brought joy and pleasure to God (vs. 19). What a beautiful thought that by living right and devoting ourselves to God puny little us can bring Him, the Almighty Creator, pleasure.
3. David lived righteously. This is defined for us in verse 20 as David making a conscious choice to live with integrity and to keep his hands from sinning. He lived with a genuine heart and sincerity toward God.
4. Verses 21 and 22 tell us that he kept God's ways, ordinances, and statutes. We must decide when we wake up each morning to follow the Word.
5. In verse 23, we learn that David was upright and blameless before God. He was always on guard to keep himself pure, free from sin and guilt. Moment by moment we must be aware and make conscious choices that follow God's ways.

What can we take away from what the Scriptures say about David's character? Loving God and obeying God go hand-in-hand. If someone truly loves God they will learn His ways, follow His ways, and keep His rules. Our love for God is first expressed through our obedience and faithfulness to Him, and as you will see in a moment there are earthly and eternal benefits for consciously choosing to live our lives this way.

10 And He rode upon a cherub [a storm] and flew [swiftly]; yes, He sped on with the wings of the wind.
11 He made darkness His secret hiding place; as His pavilion (His canopy) round about Him were dark waters and thick clouds of the skies.
12 Out of the brightness before Him there broke forth through His thick clouds hailstones and coals of fire.
13 The Lord also thundered from the heavens, and the Most High uttered His voice, amid hailstones and coals of fire.
14 And He sent out His arrows and scattered them; and He flashed forth lightnings and put them to rout.
15 Then the beds of the sea appeared and the foundations of the world were laid bare at Your rebuke, O Lord, at the blast of the breath of Your nostrils.
16 He reached from on high, He took me; He drew me out of many waters.
17 He delivered me from my strong enemy and from those who hated and abhorred me, for they were too strong for me.
18 They confronted and came upon me in the day of my calamity, but the Lord was my stay and support.
19 He brought me forth also into a large place; He was delivering me because He was pleased with me and delighted in me.

Sadly, many Christians do not fully grasp or accept this simple concept. I read a comment on Facebook recently that illustrated this in relation to the issue of homosexuality.

--Jane Doe: "Everyone sins, every single day. It shouldn't matter what a person's sexual preference is if they have a relationship with God and ask for forgiveness at the end of every day, then why judge that person's lifestyle? No one is perfect and sin is sin."

--Me: "The bottom line is that Christians are to love people, but we cannot condone sin. We go to the Bible to see what sin is. People don't have to agree with the Bible or follow it, but we believe that will cause serious problems for them in the end. 1 Cor 6:9-10, Heb 13:4, Gen 2:24. 1 Cor 7:2. Also, no one has a real relationship with God if they continually choose to live in sin. 1 John 3:8-10 'The one who practices sin is of the devil; for the devil has sinned from the beginning. The Son of God appeared for this purpose, to destroy the Works of the devil. 9 No one who is born of God practices sin, because His seed abides in him; and he cannot sin, because he is born of God. 10 By this the children of God and the children of the devil are obvious; anyone who does not practice righteousness is not of God, not the one who does not love his brother.' Also, Hebrews 10:26."

I am not going to delve into political or social issues too deeply because that is not the purpose of this book, but I have heard many people talk about getting drunk, viewing pornography, having sex outside of marriage and so forth as if it is not a big deal. They figure that God will forgive them and then they plan to sin. God will forgive sin, but willfully doing what you know is wrong is not obedience. It is not integrity or sincerity. It is not love, and if you are not living a life of love toward God then it brings to question the validity of your conversion/salvation and thus the status of your eternal destination (which is of course only to be judged by God as he examines the heart).

We have explored David's character because character is important. It will reveal its true self through our words and actions, especially during troubled times. Our character is refined and built by struggles if we respond correctly. Responses, though, are influenced by our character. To have

²⁰ The Lord rewarded me according to my righteousness (my conscious integrity and sincerity with Him); according to the cleanness of my hands has He recompensed me.
²¹ For I have kept the ways of the Lord and have not wickedly departed from my God.
²² For all His ordinances were before me, and I put not away His statutes from me.
²³ I was upright before Him and blameless with Him, ever [on guard] to keep myself free from my sin and guilt.
²⁴ Therefore has the Lord recompensed me according to my righteousness (my uprightness and right standing with Him), according to the cleanness of my hands in His sight.
²⁵ With the kind and merciful You will show Yourself kind and merciful, with an upright man You will show Yourself upright,
²⁶ With the pure You will show Yourself pure, and with the perverse You will show Yourself contrary.
²⁷ For You deliver an afflicted and humble people but will bring down those with haughty looks.
²⁸ For You cause my lamp to be lighted and to shine; the Lord my God illumines my darkness.
²⁹ For by You I can run through a troop, and by my God I can leap over a wall.
³⁰ As for God, His way is perfect! The word of the Lord is

proper responses to circumstances and people we must have proper character. Now let us look at David's actions and see how they line up with his character and how God rewards him for choosing this way of life.

Imagine David in the bottom of a desert canyon with enemies gathering on top of the high rock walls all around him. The sun is beating down on him and the sweat is streaming down his brow. He looks to the east and to the west to find a means of escape, but there is none to be found. He is distressed and is surrounded by evil men who want him dead. Torrents of ruin flood over him and his he is terrified (vs. 4). His life flashes before his eyes as he stares death in the face (vs. 5). His heart is pounding in his chest and every muscle in his aching body is tense and on the verge of either fighting to the death or collapsing.

What does David do? He looks up to the heavens and shouts out to the top of his lungs, "I love you, Lord! I trust you and take refuge in you! You are worthy to be praised! Save me from my enemies!" (vs. 2, 3, 6) What happens next is the makings of an action sequence in an adventure film, but you will have to wait a few minutes before we get to that (I hope you can handle the suspense). For now, I will give you the spoiler alert: God saved David's life with His powerful and mighty hands (vs. 16, 19). God then rewarded David because of the way he lived his life (vs. 20). David is also recompensed according to his righteousness (vs. 24). Recompense is when God compensates or pays back for loss or harm suffered. Often, He will give us more than what was lost (Zechariah 9:12, Isaiah 61:7, and Luke 6:38).

God's character is mentioned many times throughout this Psalm. The listing of his character traits is important because it directly relates to His actions toward David.

1. God is strong, and He is our strength (vs. 1).
2. He is our rock, fortress, and deliver. He is our strong tower that we can run to for safety. He is the horn of our salvation (vs. 2). Horns are emblems of power,

tested and tried; He is a shield to all those who take refuge and put their trust in Him.

31 For who is God except the Lord? Or who is the Rock save our God,

32 The God who girds me with strength and makes my way perfect?

33 He makes my feet like hinds' feet [able to stand firmly or make progress on the dangerous heights of testing and trouble]; He sets me securely upon my high places.

34 He teaches my hands to war, so that my arms can bend a bow of bronze.

35 You have also given me the shield of Your salvation, and Your right hand has held me up; Your gentleness and condescension have made me great.

36 You have given plenty of room for my steps under me, that my feet would not slip.

37 I pursued my enemies and overtook them; neither did I turn again till they were consumed.

38 I smote them so that they were not able to rise; they fell wounded under my feet.

39 For You have girded me with strength for the battle; You have subdued under me and caused to bow down those who rose up against me.

40 You have also made my enemies turn their backs to me, that I might cut off those who hate me.

dominion, glory, and fierceness, as they are the chief means of attack and defense for animals who possess them. The expression "horn of salvation," when applied to Christ, means a salvation of strength, or a strong Savior (Luke 1:69 and biblestudytools.com)

3. God is kind and merciful to those who are kind and merciful (vs. 25). He is pure and upright with those who are pure and upright. Likewise, He is opposed to or against the wicked and rebellious (vs. 26). This is an example of what David means when he said God recompensed him according to his righteousness. God follows the law of sowing and reaping (Galatians 6:7-8). What we put into our relationship with God is what we will get out of it. What we put into our lives at work, school, ministry, or relationships we will get back on earth and in eternity, whether it be good or bad.

4. Verse 30 tells us that God is perfect, and His actions are perfect. His rules are perfect, and His Word is perfect.

5. God is gentle in verse 35, and He is merciful and has a steady, unchanging, unyielding love for us in verse 50.

What can we learn from God's character as David relates it to us? We can trust Him, and He is worthy of our love. He is worthy of our loyalty and obedience and will protect us and bless us for it. So, what did God do in this Psalm to help David and cause David to write this song of praise? Now we can get back to our action sequence...

When we left David, he was surrounded, desperate, and bellowing to God for aid. David tells us that his cry went into God's very ears (vs.6). Without God's intervention David knew he would die, and it terrified him. God is sitting on His heavenly throne and hears the cry of David. He looks down upon his beloved servant and He is furious. All of a sudden, He causes a great earthquake to open up the land. Smoke fills the sky and lightning flashes all around. His voice thunders and fire spews out of the earth (vs. 8). He

41 They cried [for help], but there was none to deliver— even unto the Lord, but He answered them not.
42 Then I beat them small as the dust before the wind; I emptied them out as the dirt and mire of the streets.
43 You have delivered me from the strivings of the people; You made me the head of the nations; a people I had not known served me.
44 As soon as they heard of me, they obeyed me; foreigners submitted themselves cringingly and yielded feigned obedience to me.
45 Foreigners lost heart and came trembling out of their caves or strongholds
46 The Lord lives! Blessed be my Rock; and let the God of my salvation be exalted,
47 The God Who avenges me and subdues peoples under me,
48 Who delivers me from my enemies; yes, You lift me up above those who rise up against me; You deliver me from the man of violence.
49 Therefore will I give thanks and extol You, O Lord, among the nations, and sing praises to Your name.
50 Great deliverances and triumphs gives He to His king; and He shows mercy and steadfast love to His anointed, to David and his offspring forever.

bows the heavens and comes down in a thick dark storm cloud that covered everything (vs. 9-11). Out of His anger He sends hailstones and coals of fire and thunders against David's enemies.

In verses 12-13 the waters rise and a great flood rushes through the canyon where David stands. God reaches His very hand down and draws David out of the many waters and saves him from his enemies (vs. 16). God then causes David's light to shine and break through the darkness of the wickedness of the people who are hunting him and who are turning against His people, the Israelites. In verse 28-32, God girds David with strength and makes his way perfect. God sets David securely in a high place and his feet are firm. He is now able to progress on heights of testing and trouble without slipping (vs. 33).

God himself taught David's hand to war and held him up in His hands. Verses 34 and 35 tell us that David was no longer pressed and closed in, but he was given plenty of room (vs. 36). All his enemies were defeated, and heads of nations and foreigners submitted to David because of God (vs. 39-40 and 43-45). God avenged David and subdued people under him.

Wow! What an amazing story of how God supernaturally rescued David! Not only that, but God rewarded David, strengthened him, taught him, guided him, and gave him prestige and authority over foreign nations. He had complete victory through God in every area of his life, and he gave God the thanks and praise for it. We too can have complete victory through Christ's death on the cross.

Side Note: http://www.cbn.com/700club/features/amazing/#protection

The following are a few real-world examples of God's miracle working power in people's lives. You don't have to be a king like David to be a recipient of God's protection.

1. Kim's van was picked up by a level 3 tornado. A witness saw the van being carried above the power lines. Kim

prayed as she shielded her son on the floor of the van, and they were safely put back down on the ground.

2. Barry's doctors gave him no hope of living through the night, but he did. He was in a horrific motorcycle accident and suffered brain damage, was partially deaf, in a coma, and both retinas were detached. After awaking from the coma and much prayer, Barry felt God's presence and knew everything would be ok. He eventually gained his sight back and some of his hearing.

3. Doctors were amazed that 8-year-old Annabel was not paralyzed and had no broken bones after falling 30 feet into a hollow tree. They said Jesus must have been with her. Annabel said she saw Jesus and He told her that there would be nothing wrong with her when the firefighters got her out. On top of that, she was healed from a chronic and incurable digestive disorder.

Prayer: God, rescue me from my enemies and from anything that is coming against me. Keep your mighty hand on me and set me in high places where my feet will not slip. Give me your strength as I take refuge in you and recompense me as you did David for everything that has been lost or stolen from me by the enemy. Guide me and teach me so that I may delight you. I love you and praise you for victory in every area of my life. Amen

Week 18 Day 1 Notes for Psalm 18: Which verse stood out to you the most and why?

_____

_____

_____

_____

What important life lesson can you apply from this Psalm?

_____

_____

_____

_____

Week 18 Day 2 Devotions: Reread Psalm 18:7-15 and the following verses on God controlling and using nature.

Jeremiah 5:22 *'Do you not fear Me?' says the LORD. 'Do you not tremble [in awe] in My presence? For I have placed the sand as a boundary for the sea, An eternal decree and a perpetual barrier beyond which it cannot pass. Though the waves [of the sea] toss and break, yet they cannot prevail [against the sand ordained* *to hold them back]; Though the waves and the billows roar, yet they cannot cross over [the barrier]. [Is not such a God to be feared?]*

Deuteronomy 11:17 *or [else] the Lord's anger will be kindled and burn against you, and He will shut up the heavens so that there will be no rain and the land will not yield its fruit; and you will perish quickly from the good land which the Lord is giving you.*

Matthew 8:26 *He said to them, "Why are you afraid, you men of little faith?" Then He got up and rebuked the winds and the sea, and there was [at once] a great and wonderful calm [a perfect peacefulness].*

Based on Psalm 18, Jeremiah 5, and Deuteronomy 11, why did God use nature as an example of something He controlled and use it to punish disobedience?

_____

_____

_____

_____

What is the significance of Jesus calming the storm in Matthew 8?

_____

_____

_____

_____

Briefly describe how has He calmed a storm in your life.

_____

_____

_____

_____

Week 18 Day 3 Devotions: Reread Psalm 18:16 and the following verses on God rescuing people from water (which represents trouble).

Jonah 2:5-6 *"The waters surrounded me, to the point of death. The great deep engulfed me, Seaweed was wrapped around my head. "I descended to the [very] roots of the mountains. The earth with its bars closed behind me [bolting me in] forever, Yet You have brought up my life from the pit (death), O Lord my God.*

Matthew 14:29-31 *He said, "Come!" So Peter got out of the boat, and walked on the water and came toward Jesus. But when he saw [the effects of] the wind, he was frightened, and he began to sink, and he cried out, "Lord, save me!" Immediately Jesus extended His hand and caught him, saying to him, "O you of little faith, why did you doubt?"*

Acts 27: 14, 18, 20-25 *[14] But soon afterward a violent wind, called Euraquilo [a northeaster, a tempestuous windstorm like a typhoon], came rushing down from the island; [18] On the next day, as we were being violently tossed about by the storm [and taking on water], they began to jettison the cargo; [20] Since neither sun nor stars appeared for many days, and no small storm kept raging about us, from then on all hope of our being saved was [growing worse and worse and] gradually abandoned. [21] After they had gone a long time without food [because of seasickness and stress], Paul stood up before them and said, "Men, you should have followed my advice and should not have set sail from Crete, and brought on this damage and loss. [22] But even now I urge you to keep up your courage and be in good spirits, because there will be no loss of life among you, but only loss of the ship. [23] For this very night an angel of the God to whom I belong and whom I serve stood before me, [24] and said, 'Stop being afraid, Paul. You must stand before Caesar; and behold, God has given you [the lives of] all those who are sailing with you.' [25] So keep up your courage, men, for I believe God and have complete confidence in Him that it will turn out exactly as I have been told;*

Jonah had to be rescued from the water because he disobeyed. Peter had to be rescued because he took his eyes off Jesus and became afraid. Paul was rescued because he had to stand before Caesar and testify of Jesus' death and resurrection so that the gospel could be spread. Which of these examples do you most identify with and why?

_____

_____

_____

_____

Why do you think God rescues people from trouble even when they are disobedient or lack faith in Him?

_____

_____

_____

Week 18 Day 4 Devotions: Reread Psalm 18:19-24 and the following verses on being rewarded according to how you live your life.

1 Corinthians 3:12-15 *But if anyone builds on the foundation with gold, silver, precious stones, wood, hay, straw, each one's work will be clearly shown [for what it is]; for the day [of judgment] will disclose it, because it is to be revealed with fire, and the fire will test the quality and character and worth of each person's work. If any person's work which he has built [on this foundation, that is, any outcome of his effort] remains [and survives* *this test], he will receive a reward. But if any person's work is burned up [by the test], he will suffer the loss [of his reward]; yet he himself will be saved, but only as [one who has barely escaped] through fire.*

Romans 2:5-7 *But because of your callous stubbornness and unrepentant heart you are [deliberately] storing up wrath for yourself on the day of wrath when God's righteous judgment will be revealed. He WILL PAY BACK TO EACH PERSON ACCORDING TO HIS DEEDS [justly, as his deeds deserve]: ⁷ to those who by persistence in doing good seek [unseen but certain heavenly] glory, honor, and immortality, [He will give the gift of] eternal life.*

Luke 6:38 *Give, and it will be given to you. They will pour into your lap a good measure—pressed down, shaken together, and running over [with no space left for more]. For with the standard of measurement you use [when you do good to others], it will be measured to you in return."*

How will God determine your reward in Heaven according to 1 Corinthians 3?

_____

_____

_____

What reward does Romans 2 say that stubbornness and unrepentance will get you?

_____

_____

Looking at Luke 6, what is God's measurement for returning good back to you?

_____

_____

Week 18 Day 5 Devotion: Reread Psalm 18:29 and the following verses on overcoming the impossible with God's help.

Matthew 19:26 *But Jesus looked at them and said, "With people [as far as it depends on them] it is impossible, but with God all things are possible."*

Ephesians 3:20 *Now to Him who is able to [carry out His purpose and] do superabundantly more than all that we dare ask or think [infinitely beyond our greatest prayers, hopes, or dreams], according to His power that is at work within us,*

Matthew 17:20 *He answered, "Because of your little faith [your lack of trust and confidence in the power of God]; for I assure you and most solemnly say to you, if you have [living] faith the size of a mustard seed, you will say to this mountain, 'Move from here to there,' and [if it is God's will] it will move; and nothing will be impossible for you.*

Write down 3 different things from these verses that enable you to do the impossible.

_____

_____

_____

_____

According to Ephesians 3 and Matthew 17, why does God do more than we ask and allow mountains to be moved?

_____

_____

_____

_____

Week 18 Day 6 Devotion: Reread Psalm 18:34 and the following verses on how God prepares us for war.

Psalm 144:1-2 *Blessed be the LORD, my Rock and my great strength, Who trains my hands for war And my fingers for battle; My [steadfast] lovingkindness and my fortress, My high tower and my rescuer, My shield and He in whom I take refuge, Who subdues my people under me.*

2 Corinthians 10:3-5 *For though we walk in the flesh [as mortal men], we are not carrying on our [spiritual] warfare according to the flesh and using the weapons of man. The weapons of our warfare are not physical [weapons of flesh and blood]. Our weapons are divinely powerful for the destruction of fortresses. We are destroying sophisticated arguments and every exalted and proud thing that sets itself up against the [true] knowledge of God, and we are taking every thought and purpose captive to the obedience of Christ,*

Ephesians 6:11-17 *Put on the full armor of God [for His precepts are like the splendid armor of a heavily-armed soldier], so that you may be able to [successfully] stand up against all the schemes and the strategies and the deceits of the devil. For our struggle is not against flesh and blood [contending only with physical opponents], but against the rulers, against the powers, against the world forces of this [present] darkness, against the spiritual forces of wickedness in the heavenly (supernatural) places. Therefore, put on the complete armor of God, so that you will be able to [successfully] resist and stand your ground in the evil day [of danger], and having done everything [that the crisis demands], to stand firm [in your place, fully prepared, immovable, victorious]. So stand firm and hold your ground, HAVING TIGHTENED THE WIDE BAND OF TRUTH (personal integrity, moral courage) AROUND YOUR WAIST and HAVING PUT ON THE BREASTPLATE OF RIGHTEOUSNESS (an upright heart), and having strapped on YOUR FEET THE GOSPEL OF PEACE IN PREPARATION [to face the enemy with firm-footed stability and the readiness produced by the good news]. Above all, lift up the [protective] shield of faith with which you can extinguish all the flaming arrows of the evil one. And take THE HELMET OF SALVATION, and the sword of the Spirit, which is the Word of God.*

God prepared David for war on many occasions and from a young age, but he was also prepared for emotional and spiritual battles. God also prepares you for these battles.

What are you destroying in 2 Corinthians 10?

_____

_____

_____

_____

Why do you put on armor based on Ephesians 6?

_____

_____

_____

_____

List your spiritual weapons.

_____

_____

_____

_____

All of these weapons are equally important, otherwise God would not have given them to us. However, people struggle with different areas of their spiritual walk. **Circle** the weapon you struggle with possessing/using the most and pray that God will strengthen that area of your warfare so you can stand firm and be victorious.

Week 18 Day 7 Devotions: Reread Psalm 18:46 and the following verses on our living God.

John 6:57 *Just as the living Father sent Me, and I live because of the Father, even so the one who feeds on Me [believes in Me, accepts Me as Savior] will also live because of Me.*

Daniel 6:26 *I issue a decree that in all the dominion of my kingdom men are to [reverently] fear and tremble before the God of Daniel, For He is the living God, enduring and steadfast forever, And His kingdom is one which will not be destroyed, And His dominion will be forever.*

Revelation 1:17-18 *When I saw Him, I fell at His feet as though dead. And He placed His right hand on me and said, "Do not be afraid; I am the First and the Last [absolute Deity, the Son of God], and the Ever-living One [living in and beyond all time and space]. I died, but see, I am alive forevermore, and I have the keys of [absolute control and victory over] death and of Hades (the realm of the dead).*

Hallelujah God is alive! How do you partake in that life according to John 6?

_____

_____

Name 3 specific things that would be drastically different if America's leaders would make the same declaration as the king in Daniel 6.

_____

_____

Do not be afraid because Jesus is _____

_____ and has _____

_____

Week 19 Day 1: Psalm 19

¹ The heavens declare the glory of God; and the firmament shows and proclaims His handiwork.
² Day after day pours forth speech, and night after night shows forth knowledge.
³ There is no speech nor spoken word [from the stars]; their voice is not heard.
⁴ Yet their voice [in evidence] goes out through all the earth, their sayings to the end of the world. Of the heavens has God made a tent for the sun,
⁵ Which is as a bridegroom coming out of his chamber; and it rejoices as a strong man to run his course.
⁶ Its going forth is from the end of the heavens, and its circuit to the ends of it; and nothing [yes, no one] is hidden from the heat of it.
⁷ The law of the Lord is perfect, restoring the [whole] person; the testimony of the Lord is sure, making wise the simple.
⁸ The precepts of the Lord are right, rejoicing the heart; the commandment of the Lord is pure and bright, enlightening the eyes.
⁹ The [reverent] fear of the Lord is clean, enduring forever; the ordinances of the Lord are true and righteous altogether.
¹⁰ More to be desired are they than gold, even than much fine gold; they are sweeter

Psalm 19 is divided into three categories. First, in verses 1-6, David explains how God is revealed to all men through His wonderful creation. God so intricately made the world and all within it that His very creation declares and proclaims (announces, affirms, and broadcasts) His existence (vs.1). The very fact that day turns into night, night to day, and so forth speaks to a divine and masterful creator (vs. 2). The cycles of time and seasons effortlessly progress like a river continuously flowing into the ocean, and with each new day a quiet speech pours forth whispering, "I am here."

The stars cannot speak with audible words discernible to man; yet the very fact that they exist and shine forth night after night, year after year is clear evidence to us that there is a God. Their twinkling sings a song of praise to their Creator that reaches to the ends of the Earth (vs. 4).

Then comes the sun bright and strong (vs. 5). There is no one on earth out of its reach (vs. 6). It boldly declares to all who feel its heat, "I AM! Believe in me and you will be saved!" Paul expounds on this beautifully in Romans 1:18-20. He tells us that God's wrath is revealed from heaven against those who repress and hinder the truth. These men are wicked because God has made himself known to them in their inner consciousness, and if that wasn't enough, He is visibly evident in nature. God's power and divinity is clearly seen and able to be understood in His handiwork so that no one has an excuse or defense for denying His existence (see side note p. 124).

Yet, look at what many people have done to pervert the truth and make the truth inoperative (out of order, broken down). For example, the theory of evolution has ravaged our society and has caused people to be blinded to the truth of a divine creator.

"Since the issuance of Charles Darwin's, The Origin of Species *(1859), there has been a massive campaign to flood the 'intellectual market' with evolutionary propaganda... the theory of evolution has accelerated in influence via the media and the public school system.*

also than honey and drippings from the honeycomb.
11 Moreover, by them is Your servant warned (reminded, illuminated, and instructed); and in keeping them there is great reward.
12 Who can discern his lapses and errors? Clear me from hidden [and unconscious] faults.
13 Keep back Your servant also from presumptuous sins; let them not have dominion over me! Then shall I be blameless, and I shall be innocent and clear of great transgression.
14 Let the words of my mouth and the meditation of my heart be acceptable in Your sight, O Lord, my [firm, impenetrable] Rock and my Redeemer.

Side Note: smashinglists.com and godandscience.org

1. There are ten major theories of how life on Earth originated, creation being one of them.
2. Isaac Newton (1642-1727) "The most beautiful system of the sun, planets, and comets, could only proceed from the counsel and dominion of an intelligent and powerful Being."
3. Robert Boyle (1791-1867) *Encyclopedia Britannica* says of him: "By his will he endowed a series of Boyle lectures, or sermons, which

Today, there exists a determined campaign for the indoctrination of evolution, and millions have absorbed it into their minds..." In 1966, H. J. Muller, a prominent geneticist, circulated a statement signed by 177 biologists. It asserted that evolution is a *"scientific law which is as firmly established as the rotundity of the earth..."* However, it is not scientific law and *"There are numerous laws, e.g., the laws of thermodynamics, genetics, etc., which contradict evolutionary assertions."* (Christiancurior.com)

Since Paul tells us that God directly puts evidence in each of us and shouts out in nature that He exists, men make a conscious choice to turn from Him and believe in things such as evolution. Romans 1:21- 23 tells us that people who do this become futile and godless in their thinking. They claim to have vast knowledge and wisdom, but they are really simpletons who participate in foolish reasoning and stupid speculations. They end up worshiping creation itself or make themselves like gods because their minds become dark. If you read further in Romans chapter 1 you will see what the results of this darkness is and its consequences.

The middle part of Psalm 19 is verses 7-11. David tells us of the perfectness of God and His laws. God's ways will restore people to Him if they choose to follow them (vs. 7). There is wisdom that comes from believing in God and acknowledging Him through obedience of His laws (unlike the people Paul talked about in Romans 1). Since God is perfect and righteous, then His commandments and ordinances are as well (vs. 8 and 9). David tells us that our hearts rejoice, and our eyes are enlightened by them. They are more valuable to us than gold and sweeter to our spirits that honey (vs. 10). Because of His commandments, we learn to have reverence for the Lord, not out of fear of His wrath, but in awe of His purity and majesty.

Finally, David realizes his imperfectness and asks God to clean him up and free him from sin. Verse 12 tells us that we can even have hidden or unconscious faults and sins. Sometimes we do not even realize we are sinning. Maybe we have never been taught what gossip really is, for example, so we don't know that what we have just shared was an error.

still continue, 'for proving the Christian religion against notorious infidels...'

4. Albert Einstein was quoted by a student as to his desire to know how and why God created the world.

Prayer: God, you are awesome and marvelous. Your creation sings your praises, and I am your creation too. I praise you and testify of your goodness. I pray that you will open the eyes of those who have been deceived so that the truth of your Word will operate properly and not be hindered. I realize that without you we are all flawed but through the cross we are restored. Thank you for cleaning me up and for being my Rock and Redeemer. Amen.

Sometimes we have not not put our roots down deep enough to know and understand all of God's laws. Sometimes we speak or act in a certain way and don't realize that the root of it is pride or un-forgiveness. David prays here for God to cleanse him of all unknown lapses and faults. David then asks God to keep him from obvious or deliberate sin that can take over his life (vs. 13). He desires to be innocent, clean, and acceptable before God (vs. 14). He wants his words and thoughts to be pure because God is his Rock and Redeemer.

It is no mistake that this Psalm falls in the order we have discussed. David sees God as he examines the miraculous world around him. This causes him to reflect on who God is and the Word He has given to us to live by. He sees that the Word is without flaw, but he is not; he then sees his need for restoration and forgiveness from his redeemer.

Men must first believe that God exists, and that He rewards those who earnestly seek Him out (Hebrews 11:6). God places knowledge of Him directly in our spirit and also speaks to us every day through nature (Psalm 19 and Romans 1). Faith and trust in God's divine nature and in His commandments help us to want to follow Him and gives us wisdom. This wisdom shows us how much we need redemption and restoration. He is so perfect and we are so flawed, but all we must do to be united with Him again is to believe and ask God to forgive us. Then we will live according to the Word, and God will cause our hearts to rejoice as we lean firmly on our impenetrable Rock. Psalm 19 is the message of grace. No one is without excuse, and we all have a chance to be justified through faith in Him. Praise the Lord!

Week 19 Day 1 Notes for Psalm 19: Which verse stood out to you the most and why?

_____

_____

_____

_____

What important life lesson can you apply from this Psalm?

_____

_____

_____

_____

Week 19 Day 2 Devotions: Reread Psalm 19:1-4 and the following verses on nature declaring God's goodness and glory.

Job 12:7-10 _"Now ask the animals, and let them teach you [that God does not deal with His creatures according to their character]; And ask the birds of the air, and let them tell you; Or speak to the earth [with its many forms of life], and it will teach you; And let the fish of the sea declare [this truth] to you. "Who among all these does not recognize [in all these things that good and evil are randomly scattered throughout nature and human life]That the hand of the LORD has done this, In whose hand is the life of every living thing, And the breath of all mankind?_

Romans 1:20 _For ever since the creation of the world His invisible attributes, His eternal power and divine nature, have been clearly seen, being understood through His workmanship [all His creation, the wonderful things that He has made], so that they [who fail to believe and trust in Him] are without excuse and without defense._

Psalm 148:1-6 _Praise the LORD! Praise the LORD from the heavens; Praise Him in the heights! Praise Him, all His angels; Praise Him, all His hosts (armies)! Praise Him, sun and moon: Praise Him, all stars of light! Praise Him, highest heavens, And the waters above the heavens! Let them praise the name of the LORD, For He commanded and they were created._

All of nature declares that God exists and teaches us about His nature. The creatures, sun moon, and stars are in His hands and praise Him--show His glory. Reflect for a few moments about all you know about God through His Word, this Bible study, and your personal experience. Briefly describe one of God's attributes and how you personally see it in nature.

_____

_____

_____

Week 19 Day 3 Devotions: Reread Psalm 19:8 and the following verses on God's Word/law bringing joy.

Psalm 119:13-15 *With my lips I have told of All the ordinances of Your mouth. I have rejoiced in the way of Your testimonies, As much as in all riches. I will meditate on Your precepts And [thoughtfully] regard Your ways [the path of life established by Your precepts].*

Psalm 40:7-9 *Then I said, "Behold, I come [to the throne]; In the scroll of the book it is written of me. "I delight to do Your will, O my God; Your law is within my heart." I have proclaimed good news of righteousness [and the joy that comes from obedience to You] in the great assembly; Behold, I will not restrain my lips [from proclaiming Your righteousness], As You know, O LORD.*

Psalm 119:162 *I rejoice at Your word, as one who finds great treasure.*

What does meditating on God's Word mean to you and what does it look like in your life?

_____

_____

_____

How does David feel about God's Word in psalm 119?

_____

_____

_____

Why does David proclaim the "good news of righteousness" according to Psalm 40?

_____

_____

Week 19 Day 4 Devotions: Reread Psalm 19:8 and the following verses on God enlightening/opening your eyes.

Ephesians 1:18 *And [I pray] that the eyes of your heart [the very center and core of your being] may be enlightened [flooded with light by the Holy Spirit], so that you will know and cherish the hope [the divine guarantee, the confident expectation] to which He has called you, the riches of His glorious inheritance in the saints (God's people),*

Acts 26:18 *to open their [spiritual] eyes so that they may turn from darkness to light and from the power of Satan to God, that they may receive forgiveness and release from their sins and an inheritance among those who have been sanctified (set apart, made holy) by faith in Me.'*

2 Corinthians 3:15-17 But to this day whenever Moses is read, a veil [of blindness] lies over their heart; but whenever a person turns [in repentance and faith] to the Lord, the veil is taken away. Now the Lord is the Spirit, and where the Spirit of the Lord is, there is liberty [emancipation from bondage, true freedom].

According to Ephesians 1, what opens the eyes of your heart and why should our hearts be opened?

_____

_____

_____

_____

What does Acts 26 tell you are the benefits of having your spiritual eyes open (there are 5)?

_____

_____

What causes the veil to be taken away in 2 Corinthians 3?

_____

_____

Week 19 Day 5 Devotions: Reread Psalm 19:9-10 and the following verse about God's Word being sweet and worth more than gold.

Psalm 119:72 (103, 127) *The law from Your mouth is better to me than thousands of gold and silver pieces.*

Ezekiel 3:3 *He said to me, "Son of man, eat this scroll that I am giving you and fill your stomach with it." So I ate it, and it was as sweet as honey in my mouth.*

Jeremiah 15:16 *Your words were found and I ate them, And Your words became a joy to me and the delight of my heart; For I have been called by Your name, O LORD God of hosts.*

What are Ezekiel and Jeremiah doing to the words God has given them?

_____

What was their reaction to this?

_____

_____

_____

Ask God right now to help you be faithful at "eating" His words. As you read the Word of God, study it, meditate on it, and live it out in your daily life, you too will discover how sweet and valuable it is to you. Your spirit will begin to crave it because it brings you joy.

Week 19 Day 6 Devotions: Reread Psalm 19:12 and the following verses about hidden sin.

Isaiah 29:15 *Woe (judgment is coming) to those who [try to] deeply hide their plans from the LORD, Whose deeds are done in a dark place, and who say, "Who sees us?" or "Who knows us?"*

Psalm 90:8 *You have placed our wickedness before you, our secret sins [which we tried to conceal, You have placed] in the [revealing] light of Your presence.*

Proverbs 28:13 *He who conceals his transgressions will not prosper, but whoever confesses and turns away from his sins will find compassion and mercy.*

According to Isaiah 29 and Proverbs 28, what happens to those who conceal sin?

_____

_____

_____

What does David say exposes secret sin? _____

As you delve into the Word and love it as David did, you will be ever closer to God's heart and in His presence. This should prompt you to ask God to reveal any hidden sins or faults that need to be removed from your life, things you may not even realize are sins, because you will desire to please God and not quench the Holy Spirit working in your life.

Week 19 Day 6 Devotions: Reread Psalm 19:13 and the following verses about willful sin.

Hebrews 10:26 *For if we go on willfully and deliberately sinning after receiving the knowledge of the truth, there no longer remains a sacrifice [to atone] for our sins [that is, no further offering to anticipate],*

Matthew 6:13 *'And do not lead us into temptation, but deliver us from evil. [For Yours is the kingdom and the power and the glory forever. Amen.]'*

Romans 6:18 *And having been set free from sin, you have become the slaves of righteousness [of conformity to God's will and purpose].*

You have been _____ from sin according to Romans 6.

If you continue to willfully sin, there is no longer a _____ based on Hebrews 10.

According to Matthew 6, part of your daily prayer should be _____

_____

_____

_____

God's grace erases sin and empowers you not to sin. Let His presence and power wash over you now as you confess any deliberate sins. Put them under the blood of Jesus and rejoice in His forgiveness.

Week 20 Day 1: Psalm 20

¹ May the Lord answer you in the day of trouble! May the name of the God of Jacob set you up on high [and defend you];
² Send you help from the sanctuary and support, refresh, and strengthen you from Zion;
³ Remember all your offerings and accept your burnt sacrifice. Selah [pause, and think of that]!
⁴ May He grant you according to your heart's desire and fulfill all your plans.
⁵ We will [shout in] triumph at your salvation and victory, and in the name of our God we will set up our banners. May the Lord fulfill all your petitions.
⁶ Now I know that the Lord saves His anointed; He will answer him from His holy heaven with the saving strength of His right hand.
⁷ Some trust in and boast of chariots and some of horses, but we will trust in and boast of the name of the Lord our God.
⁸ They are bowed down and fallen, but we are risen and stand upright.
⁹ O Lord, give victory; let the King answer us when we call.

Our words have power! God created the universe and every living creature (except man) by speaking it into existence. God gave us the same creative power the moment He breathed His Spirit into us. Unfortunately, because of sin we also have destructive power in our tongues (Proverbs 18:21). Our words either bless or curse (James 3:8-10). Our words also create the atmosphere in our homes and on the job. What kind of atmosphere are you creating with your words?

Words either set angels or demons to work. Psalm 103:20 says that angels listen and obey the voice of His Word. The Bible is the Word of God, but the Word must be spoken in order for angels to act upon it. When we speak the Word of God, angels listen and perform it in our lives (Daniel 10:11-12). We also prevent angels from working on our behalf by speaking contrary to the Word of God (i.e. "I have such bad luck." "I can't do anything right." "I'm so sick." "My cancer").

Because words are so powerful, we must be conscious about what we are saying at all times. We need to create good speaking habits so that our natural reaction is to speak positively about people and situations that arise. Don't be discouraged if it takes you a while to tame your tongue or if you slip up here and there. I constantly fight this battle myself. When you catch the error, repent immediately and then speak the appropriate response. Meditating on and memorizing scripture is very important in this battle with our mouth because what is inside of us is what will emerge (Luke 6:45).

In Psalm 20, David is using his power to speak a blessing over Israel before they go to battle with Syria. As king of Israel, he has the authority and the responsibility to do this, just like we do over our lives, households, and children. A blessing is different than a prayer. Prayers are requests we ask of God, conversations with Him, or a way to praise and thank Him. They are meant to strengthen our relationship with Him. Blessings are not spoken to God but are spoken over people and acknowledge God's ability to intervene in our lives and provide for us. When we bless, we are transferring the Word of God onto that person and putting it into action.

Imagine David standing on the balcony of his palace before his soldiers and a crowd of onlookers before they march into battle. He speaks this Psalm over them with boldness and confidence because he has personally experienced what he is pronouncing over them (vs. 6). He might as well have said, "God will answer us when we face trouble. He will set us in a high place away from our enemies and will personally defend us (vs. 1). He will reach down from heaven to support, refresh, and strengthen us (vs. 2). God is faithful and will remember our sacrifices and recompense us for our righteousness (vs. 3). He will answer our prayers, grant our petitions, and cause our plans to come to fruition (vs. 4, 5). Because of salvation and the victory He brings, we will shout in triumph and will set banners high upon the walls that surround our great city in honor of His name (vs. 5)! All the nations will see these banners and will know who our God is and what He has done!"

David concludes his speech by declaring that his trust and therefore the trust of the nation is fully on God. Other nations may rely on their own strength and the strength of their earthly armies, but Israel will rely on the Almighty. Other kings will boast of their own exploits, but Israel will proudly boast of God's glory and power. Other nations are bowed down and fallen because they do not rely on God, but Israel is blessed. Israel is strong and prominent in the land as they call on God, and He will give them the victory in the battle they are about to enter.

God gives us victory in our personal battles as well. We must get as much of the Word in us as possible and start speaking out loud it over our lives and the lives of others. Our words have power, and we will be held accountable for them (Matthew 12:36). Use your words today to bless.

Week 20 Day 1 Notes for Psalm 20: Which verse stood out to you the most and why?

_____

_____

_____

_____

What important life lesson can you apply from this Psalm?

_____

_____

_____

_____

Week 20 Day 2 Devotions: Reread Psalm 20:1 and the following verses about how God is your defense.

Psalm 94:22 But the LORD has become my high tower _and_ defense, and my God the rock of my refuge.

Psalm 91:11 For He will command His angels in regard to you, to protect _and_ defend _and_ guard you in all your ways [of obedience and service].

Luke 18:7-8 And will not [our just] God defend _and_ avenge His elect [His chosen ones] who cry out to Him day and night? Will He delay [in providing justice] on their behalf? I tell you that He will defend _and_ avenge them quickly. However, when the Son of Man comes, will He find [this kind of persistent] faith on the earth?"

What is the stipulation in Psalm 91 for God defending you "in all your ways?"

_____

_____

Who does God defend based on Luke 18?

_____

_____

How will God "defend and avenge" those who cry out to Him?

_____

Week 20 Day 3 Devotions: Reread Psalm 20:2 and the following verses about God sending help from Heaven.

Matthew 4:10-11 Then Jesus said to him, "Go away, Satan! For it is written *and* forever remains written, 'YOU SHALL WORSHIP THE LORD YOUR GOD, AND SERVE HIM ONLY.'" Then the devil left Him; and angels came and ministered to Him [bringing Him food and serving Him].

Luke 22:42-43 saying, "Father, if You are willing, remove this cup [of divine wrath] from Me; yet not My will, but [always] Yours be done." Now an angel appeared to Him from heaven, strengthening Him.

Acts 5:19-20 But during the night an angel of the Lord opened the prison doors, and leading them out, he said, "Go, stand and *continue* to tell the people in the temple [courtyards] the whole message of this Life [the eternal life revealed by Christ and found through faith in Him]."

Briefly describe another example from the Bible of God sending angels to help people?

_____

_____

Have you personally experienced or know someone who has experienced having an angel intervene in a situation? If so, briefly describe it now.

_____

_____

I was hit by a work truck in a parking lot when I was a young child. I flew up into the air and skid across the asphalt. When I woke up, I asked if anyone had seen the angel sitting on the hood of the truck. If you would like to hear some testimonies on this subject, search the following title on YouTube: "700 Club Interactive: Angels Are Real and Angels on Assignment"

Week 20 Day 4 Devotions: Reread Psalm 20:3 and the following verses about God remembering your offering/sacrifice.

Hebrews 6:10 *For God is not unjust so as to forget your work and the love which you have shown for His name in ministering to [the needs of] the saints (God's people), as you do.*

Acts 10:4 *Cornelius was frightened and stared intently at him and said, "What is it, lord (sir)?" And the angel said to him, "Your prayers and gifts of charity have ascended as a memorial offering before God [an offering made in remembrance of His past blessings].*

Genesis 8:1 *And God remembered and thought kindly of Noah and every living thing and all the animals that were with him in the ark; and God made a wind blow over the land, and the waters receded.*

What does God remember in Hebrews 6 and Acts 10?

_____

_____

_____

Think about the story of Noah for a few moments. List 3 sacrifices he made for God?

_____

_____

_____

What has your sacrifice been for God?

_____

_____

_____

Week 20 Day 5 Devotions: Reread Psalm 20:4 and the following verses about desires and plans.

Psalm 37:4 *Delight yourself in the LORD, and He will give you the desires and petitions of your heart.*

Jeremiah 29:11 *For I know the plans and thoughts that I have for you,' says the LORD, 'plans for peace and well-being and not for disaster to give you a future and a hope*

Proverbs 19:21 *Many plans are in a man's mind, but it is the LORD'S purpose for him that will stand (be carried out).*

What does David say you have to do so that God will give you the "desires and petitions of your heart?"

_____

This verse goes two ways. 1. You must delight yourself in God and He will PUT appropriate desires in your heart. 2. He, after giving you godly desires, will make them come to fruition.

What are God's plans for you according to Jeremiah 29?

_____

No matter what your plans are, who's plans will prevail?

_____

Week 20 Day 6 Devotions: Reread Psalm 20:5 and the following verses about banners.

Exodus 17:15 *And Moses built an altar and named it The LORD Is My Banner;*

Song of Solomon 2:4 *"He has brought me to his banqueting place, and his banner over me is love [waving overhead to protect and comfort me].*

Psalm 60:4 *You have set up a banner for those who fear You [with awe-inspired reverence and submissive wonder—a banner to shield them from attack], A banner that may be displayed because of the truth. Selah.*

What does Solomon say God's banner does for him? _____

Why is this banner over him? _____

What does David say God's banner does for you? _____

Why is this banner over you? _____

Read the following article explaining Moses's banner: https://hannahscupboard.com/nissi/

Week 20 Day 7 Devotions: Reread Psalm 20:7 and the following verses on trusting God rather than man.

Jeremiah 17:5-6 *Thus says the LORD, "Cursed is the man who trusts in and relies on mankind, Making [weak, faulty human] flesh his strength, and whose mind and heart turn away from the LORD. "For he will be like a shrub in the [parched] desert; And shall not see prosperity when it comes, But shall live in the rocky places of the wilderness, In an uninhabited salt land.*

Psalm 118:8-9 *It is better to take refuge in the LORD than to trust in man. It is better to take refuge in the LORD than to trust in princes.*

Isaiah 31:1 *Woe (judgment is coming) to those who go down to Egypt for help, who rely on horses and trust in chariots because they are many, and in horsemen because they are very strong, but they do not look to the Holy One of Israel, nor seek and consult the LORD!*

What does Jeremiah say the consequences are of trusting in man?

_____

_____

_____

_____

_____

_____

What does Isaiah say will happen to those who rely on man and do not seek God?

_____

_____

_____

Briefly describe a time when you have personally or know someone who has trusted in man or the world instead of God and it did not turn out well.

_____

_____

_____

_____

Week 21 Day 1: Psalm 21

[1] *O Lord the king will delight in Your strength, And in Your salvation how greatly will he rejoice!*
[2] *You have given him his heart's desire,*
And You have not withheld the request of his lips. Selah.
[3] *For You meet him with blessings of good things; You set a crown of pure gold on his head.*
[4] *He asked life of You, And You gave it to him, Long life forever and ever more.*
[5] *His glory is great because of Your victory; Splendor and majesty You bestow upon him.*
[6] *For You make him most blessed [and a blessing] forever; You make him joyful with the joy of Your presence.*
[7] *For the king [confidently] trusts in the Lord, And through the loving kindness (faithfulness, goodness) of the Most High he will never be shaken.*
[8] *Your hand will reach out and defeat all your enemies; Your right hand will reach those who hate you.*
[9] *You will make them as [if in] a blazing oven in the time of your anger;*
The Lord will swallow them up in His wrath, And the fire will devour them.
[10] *Their offspring You will destroy from the earth, And*

In Psalm 21 David is praising God for saving his life and answering his prayers (vs. 1,2). David learned to trust and rely on God completely from a young age. He is confident that God's words are true and that He keeps his promises (vs. 7). Because of this, David knows that God will bless him, protect him, and bring about His divine purposes for David as king of Israel (vs. 3).

God did not have Samuel anoint David to be king at the approximated age of 15 only to have David be killed by the Philistines, Saul, Syrians, or Absalom. God's Word goes forth and does not return void. It accomplishes what it intends to accomplish (Is 55:11). In fact, David is experiencing the continuation of the covenant God made with Abram 600 years before his time. David tells us that God blessed him greatly so that he could be a blessing to others forever (vs. 6). This is what God promised Abram in Genesis 12:2, "I will make you into a great nation, and I will bless you; I will make your name great, and you will be a blessing." Isn't it amazing that God did not give up on His people or His promises over the course of time?

I would like to take a moment to talk about covenants. I am no scholar and cannot possibly delve into the deepest depths of this concept in a few short paragraphs, but I can at least mention its significance and begin you on the journey of researching it for yourself. After all, David is confident in the Lord because of His faithfulness and affirms God's blessings over himself. These two things are directly related to God making and keeping covenants.

In Hebrew, the word for covenant is berit, which means to cut. Traditional covenants required the cutting of a sacrificial animal into two parts, between which the contracting parties would each pass through the separate parts to show that they were bound to each other through the blood and death of the animal. This is where the term "cut a deal" comes from. In God's covenant with Abram it is God who commits himself and swears to keep the promise. Genesis 15:7 tells us that God appeared as a flame and was the only one to pass through the pieces. This is significant because God made

their descendants from the sons of men.
11 For they planned evil against You;
They devised a [malevolent] plot
And they will not succeed.
12 For You will make them turn their backs [in defeat]; You will aim Your bowstring [of divine justice] at their faces.
13 Be exalted, Lord, in Your strength;
We will sing and praise Your power.

Side Note:

Jeremiah 31:31-34 "Behold, the days are coming," says the Lord, "when I will make a new covenant with the house of Israel (the Northern Kingdom) and with the house of Judah (the Southern Kingdom), not like the covenant which I made with their fathers in the day when I took them by the hand to bring them out of the land of Egypt, My covenant which they broke, although I was a husband to them," says the Lord. "But this is the covenant which I will make with the house of Israel after those days," says the Lord, "I will put My law within them, and I will write it on their hearts; and I will be their God, and they will be My people. And each man will no longer teach his neighbor and his brother, saying, 'Know

a covenant with himself, not man. This covenant does not depend on man's faithfulness to keep the promise but relies fully on God's faithfulness to keep it. I want that to sink in, so pause a moment and slowly re-read that last sentence, pondering it and meditating on it. As adopted children of God and co-heirs with Christ, we are now part of that Abrahamic covenant (Ephesians 1:5, Romans 8:17, Galatians 3:7-9).

Every covenant God made in the Bible depends solely upon Him, not us. We can accept or reject the covenant. We can choose to disobey or to walk in disbelief, but His promises remain steady and eternal. No wonder David had such reverence, awe, and faith in God!

The first covenant we see is God's covenant with Noah that He would never again flood the entire world (Gen 9:8-11). The second was the Abrahamic Covenant, which we have already discussed. The next covenant was the Mosaic Covenant with which God set forth the Ten Commandments and the Jewish laws. The Davidic Covenant was God's promise that the man after His own heart, David, would live on forever, meaning that Jesus would be from the lineage of David and would rule as King in a kingdom that would never pass away (see side note).

Now, it must be noted that several of the covenants God made set forth negative consequences if the Israelites disobeyed. These are conditional covenants in that disobedience would cause a curse and the people would be scattered. However, the promise itself, though with the condition of obedience, was still unwavering because God kept that negative part of the pact as we see Israel captured and disbanded several times throughout the Old Testament.

To further study covenants let us look at some synonyms for the word: contract, agreement, commitment, guarantee, warrant, pledge, promise, bond, and indenture. The God of the universe, Creator of all things, our Master, Lord, and Father binds himself and indentures himself to us! This covenant, as foretold in Jesus' death on the cross, was the fulfillment of the covenant God made to reconcile (bring together, put to right) us to Him. Hallelujah! The Bible is

the Lord,' for they will all know Me [through personal experience], from the least of them to the greatest," says the Lord. "For I will forgive their wickedness, and I will no longer remember their sin."

Hebrews 9:15 states, "For this reason He is the Mediator *and* Negotiator of a new covenant [that is, an entirely new agreement uniting God and man], so that those who have been called [by God] may receive [the fulfillment of] the promised eternal inheritance, since a death has taken place [as the payment] which redeems them from the sins *committed* under the *obsolete* first covenant."

Prayer: Thank you, Heavenly Father, for keeping your promises. Thank you for sending Jesus to save me and for the promise and hope of eternal life with You. I pray that _____ will come to know Jesus as their Savior, so they can have victory as David did and not face your eternal judgment. In Jesus' name Amen.

full of examples of God keeping His word toward Israel, individuals, and us in the death of Jesus on the cross. We know that He does not change. Since He has a proven track record, we too can count on God keeping the many promises set forth in the Bible after Jesus' death. After all, the Bible continues from Acts to Revelations. Those books are there for a purpose, for us to stand on and live by.

Back to Psalm 21, David rejoices and has deep joy because God's presence rests on him (vs. 6). With this presence comes a deep realization of God's mercy and steadfast love. Oh, to experience the presence of the Lord; it is a weighty, yet glorious thing! We cannot be moved by the enemy or by circumstances from God's presence or His love. We can choose to walk away from His love, and many do, but He will never walk away from us.

Finally, in verses 8-13, David tells us that God will find all His enemies and consume them. This is true on two levels. God destroyed people groups who came against Israel in the Old Testament, completely wiping them off the face of the earth (vs. 10). However, this is an end time prophecy as well. The book of Revelations tells us that God will execute divine justice against all who turned away from Him (vs. 12). They will be consumed with fire as they are thrown into the lake of fire for all eternity (vs. 9).

God is patient with mankind for a time, giving us many opportunities to repent and turn to Him, but He will show His strength and power. He will be exalted, and all will bow to Him and recognize He is Lord (vs. 13).

Then He will set His eternal kingdom on Earth, the New Jerusalem, as the finale of His covenant to us (Revelation 21:1-3).

Week 21 Day 1 Notes for Psalm 21: Which verse stood out to you the most and why?

_____

_____

_____

_____

What important life lesson can you apply from this Psalm?

_____

_____

_____

_____

Week 21 day 2 Devotions: Reread psalm 21:3 and the following verses about crowns. David's crown in this verse represents the blessing of God. The picture that 2 Samuel 12:30 gives us of David being crowned is a foreshadowing of Jesus coming to reign in Revelations 14:14.

1 Corinthians 9:24-25 _Do you not know that in a race all the runners run [their very best to win], but only one receives the prize? Run [your race] in such a way that you may seize the prize and make it yours! [25] Now every athlete who [goes into training and] competes in the games is disciplined and exercises self-control in all things. They do it to win a crown that withers, but we [do it to receive] an imperishable [crown that cannot wither]._

1 Thessalonians 2:19 _For who is [the object of] our hope or joy or our victor's wreath of triumphant celebration [when we stand] in the presence of our Lord Jesus at His coming? Is it not you?_

1 Peter 5:4 _And when the Chief Shepherd (Christ) appears, you will receive the [conqueror's] unfading crown of glory._

What kind of crown will you receive based on 1 Corinthians 9?

_____

_____

The way the athlete receives his crown is the same way you receive yours. How does the athlete receive his crown?

_____

_____

What kind of crown, "victor's wreath," do you receive in 1 Thessalonians 2?

_____

_____

What kind of crown does Peter say you will receive and when will you receive it?

_____

_____

I want to encourage you to study crowns further by reading the following article http://www.gotquestions. org/heavenly-crowns.html

Week 21 day 3 Devotions: Reread Psalm 21:4 and the following verses about long life.

Psalm 91:14-16 *"Because he set his love on Me, therefore I will save him; I will set him [securely] on high, because he knows My name [he confidently trusts and relies on Me, knowing I will never abandon him, no, never]. "He will call upon Me, and I will answer him; I will be with him in trouble; I will rescue him and honor him. "With a long life I will satisfy him and I will let him see My salvation."*

Ephesians 6:2-3 HONOR *[esteem, value as precious]* YOUR FATHER AND YOUR MOTHER *[and be respectful to them]—this is the first commandment with a promise—* SO THAT IT MAY BE WELL WITH YOU, AND THAT YOU MAY HAVE A LONG LIFE ON THE EARTH.

1 John 2:25 *This is the promise which He Himself promised us—eternal life.*

God himself tells you in Psalm 91 that He gives long life for those who do what? (hint: look at the 3 things the person in these verses is doing that causes God to act)

_____

_____

What does Ephesians 6 tell you to do to have a long life? _____

The best promise about life is that God gives us the free gift of eternal life. Praise Him now for yours.

Week 21 day 4 Devotions: Reread Psalm 21:5 and the following verses about God bestowing His majesty and glory.

1 Chronicles 29:25 *The LORD highly exalted Solomon in the sight of all Israel, and bestowed on him royal majesty which had not been on any king before him in Israel.*

Ezekiel 16:14 *Then your fame went out among the nations on account of your beauty, for it was perfect because of My majesty and splendor which I bestowed on you," says the Lord GOD.*

John 17:22-23 *I have given to them the glory and honor which You have given Me, that they may be one, just as We are one; I in them and You in Me, that they may be perfected and completed into one, so that the world may know [without any doubt] that You sent Me, and [that You] have loved them, just as You have loved Me.*

Looking at these 3 verses, who gave glory and to whom was it given?

_____

_____

Why does God bestow glory and majesty on His people?

_____

_____

Week 21 day 5 Devotions: Reread Psalm 21:6 and the following verses about God blessing you to be a blessing.

Proverbs 11:25-26 *The generous man [is a source of blessing and] shall be prosperous and enriched, And he who waters will himself be watered [reaping the generosity he has sown]. The people curse him who holds back grain [when the public needs it], But a blessing [from God and man] is upon the head of him who sells it.*

2 Corinthians 9:8-11 *And God is able to make all grace [every favor and earthly blessing] come in abundance to you, so that you may always [under all circumstances, regardless of the need] have complete sufficiency in everything [being completely self-sufficient in Him], and have an abundance for every good work and act of charity. As it is written and forever remains written, "H*E *[the benevolent and generous person]* SCATTERED ABROAD, HE GAVE TO THE POOR, HIS RIGHTEOUSNESS ENDURES FOREVER!" *Now He who provides seed for the sower and bread for food will provide and multiply your seed for sowing [that is, your resources] and increase the harvest of your righteousness [which shows itself in active goodness, kindness, and love]. You will be enriched in every way so that you may be generous, and this [generosity, administered] through us is producing thanksgiving to God [from those who benefit].*

Luke 12:48 *…From everyone to whom much has been given, much will be required; and to whom they entrusted much, of him they will ask all the more.*

What are promises described in Proverbs 11 and 2 Corinthians 9?

_____

_____

_____

_____

What are the blessings dependent upon in these 3 verses?

_____

_____

_____

_____

Week 21 day 6 Devotions: Reread Psalm 21:6 and the following verses about being joyful in God's presence.

Jude 24-25 *Now to Him who is able to keep you from stumbling or falling into sin, and to present you unblemished [blameless and faultless] in the presence of His glory with triumphant joy and unspeakable delight, to the only God our Savior, through Jesus Christ our Lord, be glory, majesty, dominion, and power, before all time and now and forever. Amen.*

1 Thessalonians 3:9 (NIV) *How can we thank God enough for you in return for all the joy we have in the presence of our God because of you?*

Psalm 16:11 *You will show me the path of life; In Your presence is fullness of joy; In Your right hand there are pleasures forevermore.*

Triumphant joy, unspeakable delight, fullness of joy, pleasures forevermore—these are what you can expect when abiding in God's presence!

Briefly describe a time when you experienced the greatest joy you have ever experienced in your life.

_____

_____

_____

Our greatest moments of joy cannot compare to the joy of being in the presence of God! I encourage you to find a quiet moment and place each day, pump up the worship music, and bask in His presence.

Week 21 day 7 Devotions: Reread Psalm 21:13 and the following verse about God being exalted.

<u>**Isaiah 6:1**</u> *[Isaiah's Vision] In the year that King Uzziah died, I saw [in a vision] the Lord sitting on a throne, high and exalted, with the train of His royal robe filling the [most holy part of the] temple.*

Isaiah 25:1 *O LORD, You are my God; I will exalt You, I will praise and give thanks to Your name; For You have done miraculous things,* Plans *formed long, long ago, [fulfilled] with perfect faithfulness.*

<u>**Isaiah 57:15**</u> *For the high and exalted One He who inhabits eternity, Whose name is Holy says this, "I dwell on the high and holy place, But also with the contrite and humble in spirit In order to revive the spirit of the humble And to revive the heart of the contrite [overcome with sorrow for sin].*

Why is God exalted in Isaiah 6? _____

Why is God exalted in Isaiah 25? _____

Who does our exalted, eternal king choose to dwell with in Isaiah 57? _____

Why does He dwell with them? _____

How does knowing that God wants to revive your spirit, if you are humble and contrite, make you feel (what does revive mean or what would it look like to you in your life?)

_____

_____

_____

_____

Week 22 Day 1: Psalm 22

[1] My God, my God, why have You forsaken me? Why are You so far from helping me, and from the words of my groaning?
[2] O my God, I call out by day, but You do not answer; And by night, but I find no rest nor quiet.
[3] But You are holy, O You who are enthroned in [the holy place where] the praises of Israel [are offered].
[4] In You our fathers trusted [leaned on, relied on, and were confident]; They trusted and You rescued them.
[5] They cried out to You and were delivered; They trusted in You and were not disappointed or ashamed.
[6] But I am [treated as] a worm [insignificant and powerless] and not a man; I am the scorn of men and despised by the people.
[7] All who see me laugh at me and mock me; They [insultingly] open their lips, they shake their head, saying,
[8] "He trusted and committed himself to the Lord, let Him save him.
Let Him rescue him, because He delights in him."
[9] Yet You are He who pulled me out of the womb; You made me trust when on my mother's breasts.

David most likely wrote this Psalm when his son Absalom had betrayed him and sent him fleeing for his life. If you have ever felt the sting of betrayal, then you know the heartache David is expressing in this Psalm. He has cried out to a God he knows, loves dearly, and trusts but has found no reprieve from the circumstance he faces or from the grief in his heart (vs. 1,2). He has cried aloud so long that he does not even have words left to speak, so he groans.

Have you ever been in a place like this before where you were so perplexed and distraught about a situation that you did not have words to express your heart's cry? I have. Take comfort in knowing what David tells us next in verses 3-5. Even though David felt that God had abandoned him (vs. 1), he knew deep down that it was impossible because God is holy (vs. 3). There is no evil in God, only goodness, so David reminds himself of God's covenant keeping with his forefathers. Though deliverance did not always come quickly, God did not allow them to be ashamed, confounded, or disappointed forever (vs. 5). Therefore, God would not allow David and will not allow us to be disgraced, bewildered, or disheartened forever.

No matter what is happening on the outside, God dwells in us. He inhabits (resides, makes His home) in our praises (vs. 3). Our spirit is the innermost part of our being and is like the holy of holies in the tabernacle where God dwelt among the Israelites. This is where we offer our genuine sacrifice of praise to God. It is in those moments of deepest sorrow, pain, grief etc. where it truly feels like a sacrifice to allow one note of praise to come from your lips. It may be just a whisper or even a whimper as tears stream down your cheeks, but God sees it. He hears and it is like sweet incense to His nostrils. The song becomes like a prayer or worship to Him and will change your heart in the midst of the darkness (Hebrews 13:15, Revelation 8:4, and Psalm 141:2).

When our circumstances cause our mind, body, and emotions to falter, our spirit can still praise Him in the storm. This praise will eventually manifest on the outside and bring us victory as we lean on and rely on God in

¹⁰ *I was cast upon You from birth; From my mother's womb You have been my God.*
¹¹ *Do not be far from me, for trouble is near; And there is no one to help.*
¹² *Many [enemies like] bulls have surrounded me; Strong bulls of Bashan have encircled me.*
¹³ *They open wide their mouths against me, Like a ravening and a roaring lion.*
¹⁴ *I am poured out like water, And all my bones are out of joint.*
My heart is like wax; It is melted [by anguish] within me.
¹⁵ *My strength is dried up like a fragment of clay pottery; And my [dry] tongue clings to my jaws; And You have laid me in the dust of death.*
¹⁶ *For [a pack of] dogs have surrounded me; A gang of evildoers has encircled me, They pierced my hands and my feet.*
¹⁷ *I can count all my bones; They look, they stare at me.*
¹⁸ *They divide my clothing among them And cast lots for my [b]garment.*
¹⁹ *But You, O Lord, do not be far from me; O You my help, come quickly to my assistance.*
²⁰ *Rescue my life from the sword, My only life from the paw of the dog (the executioner).*

complete confidence (vs. 4). David literally faced mocking (vs. 7), deadly foes (vs.12, 13), and loss of strength (vs. 11, 14, 15), but he is saved and declares God's name in the midst of many witnesses (vs. 21, 22). Yet, beyond the story of David's trouble and sorrow in Psalm 22 lies a much deeper picture for us to view. I want to encourage you to read through the rest of this study slowly and reverently and to re-read each verse of the Psalm as I reference it. Meditate on it and close your eyes to picture each step of suffering bore for you because, as you will see, this Psalm describes the suffering of Jesus on the cross exactly, beginning with the garden of Gethsemane.

Jesus prayed in the garden the night before He was to be crucified. He prayed so fervently for God to take this destiny from Him that His sweat turned to blood (Luke 22:44). The amount of physical and emotional stress required to cause the blood vessels around the sweat glands to burst is immeasurable, but it has been documented by physicians. Then, as Jesus hung in agony on the cross taking our sin and shame upon himself, He cried out verse one of this very Psalm, "My God, my God, why have you forsaken me?" Matthew 27:46. God had to turn His holy face away from His precious son because that is what sin does, it separates us from God. Consider the following description of Psalm 22:1-2 from an excerpt of a sermon by Charles Spurgeon:

Hell itself has for its fiercest flame the separation of the soul from God. "Forsaken:" if thou hadst chastened I might bear it, for thy face would shine; but to forsake me utterly, ah! why is this? "Me:" thine innocent, obedient, suffering Son, why leavest thou me to perish?...The Man of Sorrows had prayed until his speech failed him, and he could only utter moanings and groanings as men do in severe sicknesses, like the roarings of a wounded animal. To what extremity of grief was our Master driven? What strong crying and tears were those which made him too hoarse for speech! What must have been his anguish to find his own beloved and trusted Father standing afar off, and neither granting help nor apparently hearing prayer!... Yet there was reason for all this which those who rest in Jesus as their Substitute well know... For our prayers to appear to be unheard is no new trial, Jesus felt it before us, and it is observable that he still held fast his

21 Save me from the lion's mouth;
From the horns of the wild oxen You answer me.
22 I will tell of Your name to my countrymen; In the midst of the congregation I will praise You.
23 You who fear the Lord [with awe-inspired reverence], praise Him!
All you descendants of Jacob, honor Him. Fear Him [with submissive wonder], all you descendants of Israel.
24 For He has not despised nor detested the suffering of the afflicted; Nor has He hidden His face from him; But when he cried to Him for help, He listened.
25 My praise will be of You in the great assembly. I will pay my vows [made in the time of trouble] before those who [reverently] fear Him.
26 The afflicted will eat and be satisfied;
Those who [diligently] seek Him and require Him [as their greatest need] will praise the Lord.
May your hearts live forever!
27 All the ends of the earth will remember and turn to the Lord,
And all the families of the nations will bow down and worship before You,
28 For the kingship and the kingdom are the Lord's and He rules over the nations.

believing hold on God... for amid the hurry and horror of that dismal day he ceased not his cry, even as in Gethsemane he had agonized all through the gloomy night. Our Lord continued to pray even though no comfortable answer came... No daylight is too glaring, and no midnight too dark to pray in; and no delay or apparent denial, however grievous, should tempt us to forbear from importunate pleading.

As we move to verse 6, we see that Jesus was mocked and despised by the very people who had ushered him into the city the week before on what we call Palm Sunday (Matthew 27:43). He was treated as a worm, "So trodden under foot, trampled on, maltreated, buffeted and spit upon, mocked and tormented, as to seem more like a worm than a man. Behold what great contempt hath the Lord of Majesty endured, that his confusion may be our glory; his punishment our heavenly bliss!" (Spurgeon) The people then sarcastically shouted at Jesus telling him to save himself. If he was truly the son of God surely God would hear His cry and deliver Him (vs. 7,8 and. Matthew 27:39, 43). However, Jesus' obedience and love for us held Him to the cross more securely than the 7-inch iron spikes in his hands and feet (vs. 16). Once on the cross, Jesus did not ask for His destiny to change or to be rescued. What He wanted most was for His father, in whom He trusted and loved, to be near Him (vs. 9-11)

In verses 14 – 17, we see what Jesus' physical body went through on the cross. His strength and energy were gone like water being poured out of a pitcher onto the ground. His body had been stretched to the limit as his arms and legs were stretched to be fixed to the cross. His joints were jolted out of place as the cross was raised and dropped violently into the hole dug to keep it upright. His heart physically melted under the anguish of his sufferings due to tremendous blood loss and gravity pulling down on every organ. However, His heart anguished too as the weight of the world was placed on His spiritual shoulders.

Jesus suffered extreme thirst so that his tongue stuck to the roof of His mouth and His jaws locked (vs. 15 and John 19:28). His bones could be counted by onlookers due

²⁹ *All the prosperous of the earth will eat and worship; All those who go down to the dust (the dead) will bow before Him, even he who cannot keep his soul alive.*
³⁰ *Posterity will serve Him; They will tell of the Lord to the next generation.*
³¹ *They will come and declare His righteousness To a people yet to be born—that He has done it [and that it is finished].*

Side Note:

For more about Jesus' physical suffering on the cross visit the following sites.
http://www.catholiceducation.org/en/controversy/common-misconceptions/the-facts-of-crucifixion.html and
http://www.cbn.com/spirituallife/onlinediscipleship/easter/a_physician's_view_of_the_crucifixion_of_jesus_christ.aspx?mobile=false

Prayer: God, I cry out to you, and I know that you hear me even when I cannot see above the waves. I trust you to take care of me and my circumstances because I know you are good and faithful. I take my eyes off myself and my troubles and reverently turn them to you alone. I know that you, Jesus, have felt and experienced the same and even more suffering than I have faced or face right now. Thank you for

to being stretched out, loss of blood, and dehydration (vs. 17); all the while, soldiers gambled for his clothes (John 19:23,24). All this horror was experienced for you and for me because of our sin.

Verses 22-31 are not just about what David experience in his lifetime. They were a snapshot of what took place after Jesus' death and resurrection when the disciples began to preach the gospel (vs. 30, 31). Their faithfulness in teaching and spreading the good news of what Jesus had done to take away our sins and unite us with God once more spread through hundreds of generations and will continue until Christ returns.

Verses 26-29 go even further into the future and briefly tell us what will happen after the second coming of Christ. The poor and afflicted will be fed and satisfied. Those who seek God and require Him as their greatest need will praise Him forever (vs. 26). "Your spirit shall not fail through trial… Immortal joy shall be your portion…They who eat at Jesus' table will receive the fulfillment of the promise, 'Whosoever eateth of this bread shall live forever'." (Spurgeon)

Every person in heaven and earth will turn to God and bow down to worship Him (vs. 27,29). Jesus will be our ruler and His kingdom will be on Earth (vs. 28 and Daniel 2:44). The plans of God will finally come to fruition. What was bought and paid for on the cross was finished right then and there in the spirit realm, and it will be finally finished on earth as John gave an account in Revelations. Jesus has done it! Rejoice! Declare this message to all that IT IS FINISHED! (John 19:30).

sacrificing yourself for me and for suffering in my place. I lift you high and honor you, for you are worthy to be praised! Yours is the victory and I share in that victory because of the cross. I rejoice because every sin is finished, every sickness is finished, death is finished, every burden and shame is finished! Thank you! Hallelujah! Amen

Week 22 Day 1 Notes for Psalm 22: Which verse stood out to you the most and why?

_____

_____

_____

_____

What important life lesson can you apply from this Psalm?

_____

_____

_____

_____

Week 22 Day 2 Devotions: Reread Psalm 22:1-2 and the following verses about God not hearing or answering prayer

James 4:3 _You ask [God for something] and do not receive it, because you ask with wrong motives [out of selfishness or with an unrighteous agenda], so that [when you get what you want] you may spend it on your [hedonistic] desires._

James 1:6-8 _But he must ask [for wisdom] in faith, without doubting [God's willingness to help], for the one who doubts is like a billowing surge of the sea that is blown about and tossed by the wind. For such a person ought not to think or expect that he will receive anything [at all] from the Lord, being a double-minded man, unstable and restless in all his ways [in everything he thinks, feels, or decides]._

Isaiah 59:1-2 _Behold, the LORD's hand is not so short That it cannot save, Nor His ear so impaired That it cannot hear. But your wickedness has separated you from your God, and your sins have hidden His face from you so that He does not hear._

David was in distress and felt as though God was not listening. In David's case, he had done nothing wrong but still felt as though his prayers for help were not being answered. However, there are times when there is a reason behind unanswered prayers. What 3 things hinder prayer in the verses above?

_____

_____

Which of these things have you struggled the most with and why?

_____

_____

_____

Week 22 Day 3 Devotions: Reread Psalm 22:4-5 and the following examples of God answering prayer.

Exodus 32:11-14 *But Moses appeased and entreated the L*ORD *his God, and said, "L*ORD*, why does Your anger burn against Your people whom You have brought out of the land of Egypt with great power and a mighty hand? Why should the Egyptians say, 'With evil [intent] their God brought them out to kill them in the mountains and destroy them from the face of the earth'? Turn away from Your burning anger and change Your mind about harming Your people. Remember Abraham, Isaac, and Israel (Jacob), Your servants to whom You swore [an oath] by Yourself, and said to them, 'I will multiply your descendants as the stars of the heavens, and all this land of which I have spoken I will give to your descendants, and they shall inherit it forever.'" So the L*ORD *changed His mind about the harm which He had said He would do to His people.*

Isaiah 38:1-5 *In those days Hezekiah [king of Judah] became sick and was at the point of death. And Isaiah the prophet, the son of Amoz, came to him and said, "For the L*ORD *says this, 'Set your house in order and prepare a will, for you shall die; you will not live.'" Then Hezekiah turned his face to the wall and prayed to the L*ORD*, and said, "Please, O L*ORD*, just remember how I have walked before You in faithfulness and truth, and with a whole heart [absolutely devoted to You], and have done what is good in Your sight." And Hezekiah wept greatly. Then the word of the L*ORD *came to Isaiah, saying, "Go and say to Hezekiah, 'For the L*ORD*, the God of David your father says this, "I have heard your prayer, I have seen your tears; listen carefully, I will add fifteen years to your life.*

1 Kings 18:37-39 *Answer me, O L*ORD*, answer me, so that this people may know that You, O L*ORD*, are God, and that You have turned their hearts back [to You]." Then the fire of the L*ORD *fell and consumed the burnt offering and the wood, and even the stones and the dust; it also licked up the water in the trench. When all the people saw it, they fell face downward; and they said, "The L*ORD*, He is God! The L*ORD*, He is God!"*

What was the prayer God answered for Moses and why?

_____

_____

What prayer did God answer for Hezekiah and why?

_____

_____

What prayer did God answer for Elijah and why?

_____

_____

As you can see, there are different reasons to pray and different reasons why God answers prayer. Don't give up. Remind God of His promises by quoting scripture. Pray for protection for your nation, pray for yourself, and pray for the salvation of others.

Week 22 day 4 devotions: Reread Psalm 22: 6-8 and the following verse about being mocked because of your faith.

Luke 6:22 *Blessed [morally courageous and spiritually alive with life-joy in God's goodness] are you when people hate you, and exclude you [from their fellowship], and insult you, and scorn your name as evil because of [your association with] the Son of Man.*

1 Peter 4:14 *If you are insulted and reviled for [bearing] the name of Christ, you are blessed [happy, with life-joy and comfort in God's salvation regardless of your circumstances], because the Spirit of glory and of God is resting on you [and indwelling you—He whom they curse, you glorify].*

2 Corinthians 12:10 *So I am well pleased with weaknesses, with insults, with distresses, with persecutions, and with difficulties, for the sake of Christ; for when I am weak [in human strength], then I am strong [truly able, truly powerful, truly drawing from God's strength].*

Look at Luke 6 and 1 Peter 4, write down the 2 definitions of blessed that you see in the brackets.

_____

_____

Why does Peter say you are blessed even though you are being insulted and hated?

_____

_____

What does strong mean in 2 Corinthians 12?

_____

_____

List 3 of your main weaknesses.

_____

_____

Give those weaknesses to God right now and draw from His strength to accomplish whatever His purpose is for your life.

Week 22 Day 5 Devotions: Reread Psalm 22: 9-11 and the following verse about knowing God like a child and from childhood.

Mark 10:15-16 *I assure you and most solemnly say to you, whoever does not receive and welcome the kingdom of God like a child will not enter it at all." And He took the children [one by one] in His arms and blessed them [with kind, encouraging words], placing His hands on them.*

Matthew 19:14 *But He said, "Leave the children alone, and do not forbid them from coming to Me; for the kingdom of heaven belongs to such as these."*

Psalm 78:5-7 *For He established a testimony (a specific precept) in Jacob and appointed a law in Israel, Which He commanded our fathers That they should teach to their children [the great facts of God's transactions with Israel], That the generation to come might know them, that the children still to be born May arise and recount them to their children, That they should place their confidence in God and not forget the works of God, but keep His commandments,*

The verses above from Mark 10 and Matthew 19 are a recounting of the same story when Jesus told the disciples to allow the children to come to Him. The term "childlike faith" is often used in reference to these verses. What does it mean to have childlike faith?

_____

_____

_____

Why does Jesus say that you must come to God like a child in order to enter Heaven?

_____

_____

In psalm 78, why should you teach children about God?

_____

_____

Week 22 Day 6 Devotions: Reread Psalm 22: 14-15 and the following examples of being in distress.

Lamentations 1:20 *"See, O LORD, how distressed I am! My spirit is deeply disturbed; My heart is overturned within me and cannot rest, For I have been very rebellious. In the street the sword kills and bereaves; In the house there is [famine, disease and] death!*

Job 1:19-20 *and suddenly, a great wind came from across the desert, and struck the four corners of the house, and it fell on the young people and they died, and I alone have escaped to tell you."*

Then Job got up and tore his robe and shaved his head [in mourning for the children], and he fell to the ground and worshiped [God].

Jeremiah 8:18 *Oh, that I (Jeremiah) could find comfort from my sorrow [for my grief is beyond healing], My heart is sick and faint within me!*

Life can bring great distress in many forms and for many reasons. In Psalm 22 David has been betrayed by his son and run out of the city. In Lamentations 1, the prophet Jeremiah is distressed because Jerusalem and Judea have been attacked and destroyed by Babylon. In Jeremiah 8 he is grieving over Israel's sin and God's impending judgment. Job tears his clothes and mourns over the death of all his children. Is there something distressing you today? Take heart because God takes care of his own. David and Job were restored, and God used and protected Jeremiah.

What were the responses of the people to their distress in the examples above?

_____

_____

Briefly describe a distressing situation you are in or have experienced and how you can or did overcome it?

_____

_____

_____

Remember to share your heartaches and subsequent victories with people so they can have hope.

Week 22 Day 7 Devotions: Reread Psalm 22:14-18 and the following verses on the crucifixion of Christ.

Mark 14:65 *And some began to spit on Him, and to blindfold Him, and to beat Him with their fists, and to say to Him, "Prophesy [by telling us who hit you]!" Then the officers took custody of Him and struck him in the face.*

Matthew 27:28-31 *They stripped him and put a scarlet robe on Him [as a king's robe]. And after twisting together a crown of thorns, they put it on His head, and put a reed in His right hand [as a scepter]. Kneeling before Him, they ridiculed Him, saying, "Hail (rejoice), King of the Jews!" They spat on Him, and took the reed and struck Him repeatedly on the head. After they finished ridiculing Him, they stripped Him of the scarlet robe and put His own clothes on Him, and led Him away to crucify Him.*

Isaiah 52:14 *Just as many were astonished and appalled at you, My people, So His appearance was marred more than any man And His form [marred] more than the sons of men.*

What is the most physically painful situation you have ever experienced?

_____

How did the pain affect you mentally and emotionally?

_____

_____

_____

List the actions taken physically against Jesus in Mark 14 and Matthew 27.

_____

_____

_____

He endured all these and more for you! Thank Him and praise Him for taking your place on the cross. Share the knowledge and joy of salvation with someone today.

Week 23 Day 1: Psalm 23

The Lord is my Shepherd [to feed, to guide and to shield me], I shall not want.
² He lets me lie down in green pastures;
He leads me beside the still and quiet waters.
³ He refreshes and restores my soul (life); He leads me in the paths of righteousness for His name's sake.
⁴ Even though I walk through the [sunless] valley of the shadow of death, I fear no evil, for You are with me; Your rod [to protect] and Your staff [to guide], they comfort and console me.
⁵ You prepare a table before me in the presence of my enemies. You have anointed and refreshed my head with oil; My cup overflows.
⁶ Surely goodness and mercy and unfailing love shall follow me all the days of my life, And I shall dwell forever [throughout all my days] in the house and in the presence of the Lord.

Side Note: staff and rod http://www.antipas.org/commentaries/articles/shepherd_psa23/shepherd_07.html

As I read this Psalm, there's a quiet reserved tone in David's voice much like that of the hymn "It Is Well." He is neither crying out to

As I sit down to write about this, tears begin to well up in my eyes. I read Psalm 23 and wrote a few thoughts down about a month ago. Before that I had written nearly every day through June and July, but I could not bring myself to continue until today.

It is no coincidence that my study of Psalms brought me to this particular one at this time in my life. You see, the day after I started working on it there was a shift in my father-in-law's condition. My mother-in-law, two sisters-in-law, and I had been taking care of our father day and night for over a month. As he lay in a hospital bed in their living room, we fought for him to live.

We had walked through the valley of the shadow of death with him four years ago and saw God work a miracle in him. Three doctors told us he would die, but God had shown each of us that it was not his time. We pressed in and stood on the Word. He made it through the night and went home a week later with no explanation from the doctors as to how or why my father-in-law was still here. He had been diagnosed with carcinoid tumors four years before that incident, so they thought the tumors had won. They were wrong, so when we were told the same thing again this summer we stood firmly on the Word of God for miracle once again.

When the shift happened, we could all feel Papa letting go. The next day I had a rare few moments alone with him early in the quiet of the morning. I told him how much I loved him and how wonderful an example he was to all of us– a godly example. I whispered Psalm 23 in his ear, half as a prayer of restoration and life in this world with us, but also knowing that he would be fully restored and walk beside still waters should he be called home. I told him it was his choice to make; we would fight for him, or we would let him go, and we would be ok.

My daughter, 12 at the time, came over shortly after and played a song from my phone by Bethel Music, "Grander earth has quaked before, moved by the sound of His voice. Seas that are shaken and stirred can be calmed and broken for my regard. Through it all, through it all my eyes are on

God nor rejoicing loudly. This Psalm was used by the Jewish people as a comfort during the deepest despairing times. This is partly due to the image it depicts of God as our shepherd. How can we find comfort in our darkest moments if we cannot trust what David tells us about God in Psalm 23? How can we trust that all the things in this Psalm are true if we do not understand fully what it means for God to be our shepherd?

It may be difficult for our industrialized selves to understand fully what a shepherd represents unless you are from an agricultural background, but in David's time, being a shepherd was an important job. The Israelites had been shepherds for generations. Sheep were a vital part of their economy, a source of wool for clothing, and meat for the table (Don't lose sight of verse 1 of this Psalm as you continue reading).

The shepherd guarded his family's livelihood and food supply with his life. He was constantly exposed to the elements and to predators such as wolves, jackals, lions, bobcats, and leopards armed only with a staff, a rod, and a sling for protection.

You. Through it all, through it all, it is well...so let it go my soul and trust in Him. The waves and wind still know His name...It is well with my soul..." He passed away an hour or so later. I cry every time I hear that song because I never expected to have to be "well" with the death of such a precious and vital person in our family's life.

Many situations, even if not life-threatening, can cause us to find ourselves in a deep and sunless valley where green pastures and still waters cannot be seen in the natural, but I am here to tell you that those things do come into view eventually if you wait on and trust in the Lord as we have learned from so many Psalms already. One of my closest friends went through a long and terrifying valley with her husband who battled depression and alcohol- he has since been delivered and God is using him. Another dear friend had a devastating miscarriage- she is blessed with children now. Yet another's valley was the mental illness of a parent, who is doing very well now, and another's was a horrible ex-husband and a wayward daughter (we are still working on them, but the desperation and darkness are over).

Psalm 23 has different meanings for people depending on the valley they face, but the message remains the same no matter who you are. The Lord is our shepherd; therefore, we lack for nothing (vs. 1). He leads us to good places if we will allow Him to do so (vs. 2). He restores our emotions, our very inner selves (vs. 3). He fiercely guards us (vs. 4) and causes us to be at peace, even in the midst of the enemy (vs. 5).

Our valleys and "shadows of death" can be markedly different from other people's experiences, but God can refresh us time and time again. He has enough mercy and grace for each of us each day, through each valley we go through in our lives (Lamentations 3:22-23). Many times we have to follow Him in the dark, but He will bring the light again and restore us a promised in verse 3. Sometimes this process takes longer than we would like it too, but I am here on the "restoring of the soul" side to encourage you to hang on.

The rod was used to protect by warding off predators and to discipline sheep that wandered off. What you may not know is that it was also used to examine the sheep as they entered the fold. It represents, "…coming under the owner's control and authority, but also to be subject to his most careful, intimate and firsthand examination. A sheep that passed 'under the rod' was one which had been counted and looked over with great care to make sure all was well with it." The image painted here by David is that God is our divine protector, corrector, and most careful and intimate leader.

The staff was used to guide sheep, lift lambs to return them to their mothers and to safety, and a support to the shepherd when tired or going through rocky terrain. God not only uses His "staff," He *IS* our staff. He is our lifter to nurturing and safety. He is our support when we grow weary or struggle.

The shepherd's days consisted of moving the flock from the small stone walled or temporary thicket enclosure (the sheepfold) to fresh, calm water.

Sheep prefer to drink from water that is not flowing strongly, nor water that is stagnant. God, as our

Psalm 23 is a promise for this world through the length of our days but also for the life to come as we enter into eternity with Him. We will be forever in green pastures (vs. 2), forever refreshed and restored (vs. 3), and completely and forever in God's presence (vs. 6). We will never again fear, never again be in darkness, and never again be in death's shadow (vs. 4). Surely only goodness, mercy, and unfailing love will be ours forever (vs. 6)!

shepherd, does not lead us to threatening water or stale, unhealthy water, but to water that refreshes and gives life. The shepherd also moved the flock to good grazing land. Grass is a sheep's main sustenance, which is needed to have healthy sheep for reproduction and meat. Much of Israel's terrain is dry and barren, with desserts and wildernesses in abundance, so finding lush, green pastureland to rest in while the flock grazed would have been a tremendous blessing. Each of us needs a place to escape the noise and turmoil of this fallen world where we can be physically, mentally, and spiritually rejuvenated. Only our Great Shepherd can lead us to such a place.

Prayer: Father, when I cannot see, when my heart wants to give up, when fear tries to creep in and enemies rise up against me, I will remember You as my Great Shepherd. Thank You for your correction and direction. Thank You for your care and intimate knowledge of me. Thank You for support and nurturing, and safety. Refresh me, restore me, and give me divine rest. May I dwell in Your beautiful and powerful presence all of our days on this earth and forevermore. Amen

Week 23 Day 1 Notes for Psalm 23: Which verse stood out to you the most and why?

_____

_____

_____

_____

What important life lesson can you apply from this Psalm?

_____

_____

_____

Week 23 Day 2 Devotions: Reread Psalm 23:1 and the following verses about provision.

Psalm 34:9-10 _O [reverently] fear the LORD, you His saints (believers, holy ones); For to those who fear Him there is no want. The young lions lack [food] and grow hungry, but they who seek the LORD will not lack any good thing._

Philippians 4:19 _And my God will liberally supply (fill until full) your every need according to His riches in glory in Christ Jesus._

Luke 12:29-32 _So as for you, do not seek what you will eat and what you will drink; nor have an anxious and unsettled mind. For all the [pagan] nations of the world greedily seek these things; and your [heavenly] Father [already] knows that you need them. But [strive for and actively] seek His kingdom, and these things will be given to you as well. Do not be afraid and anxious, little flock, for it is your Father's good pleasure to give you the kingdom._

Who does David say will not want or lack in Psalm 34?

_____

_____

What should you be seeking after in Luke 12? _____

What promises do you see in Philippians 4 and Luke 12?

_____

_____

Week 23 Day 3 Devotions: Reread Psalm 23:2-3 and the following verses about how He leads and guides you.

Isaiah 40:11 *He will protect His flock like a shepherd, He will gather the lambs in His arm, He will carry them in His bosom; He will gently and carefully lead those nursing their young.*

Psalm 78:52-53 *But God led His own people forward like sheep and guided them in the wilderness like [a good shepherd with] a flock. He led them safely, so that they did not fear; But the sea engulfed their enemies.*

Revelation 7:17 *for the Lamb who is in the center of the throne will be their Shepherd, and He will guide them to springs of the waters of life; and God will wipe every tear from their eyes [giving them eternal comfort]."*

There is a promise for God to lead His people as a shepherd. Look back at the side note on shepherds and the 3 verses above. What 2 qualities of a shepherd stand out most to you and why?

_____

_____

_____

_____

Briefly explain how God has exhibited the characteristics of a shepherd in your life.

_____

_____

_____

_____

Week 23 Day 4 Devotions: Reread Psalm 23:3 and the following verses about being refreshed.

Jeremiah 31:25 *For I [fully] satisfy the weary soul, and I replenish every languishing and sorrowful person."*

Acts 3:19 *So repent [change your inner self—your old way of thinking, regret past sins] and return [to God—seek His purpose for your life], so that your sins may be wiped away [blotted out, completely erased], so that times of refreshing may come from the presence of the Lord [restoring you like a cool wind on a hot day];*

2 Timothy 1:16 *The Lord grant mercy to the family of Onesiphorus, because he often **refresh**ed me and showed me kindness [comforting and reviving me like fresh air] and he was not ashamed of my chains [for Christ's sake];*

According to Acts 3, what do you have to do so that you can be refreshed? _____

How is refreshing defined in Acts 3? _____

As God refreshes us, we in turn are to refresh others as Onesiphorus refreshed Paul. List 3 specific ways you can refresh someone today.

_____

_____

Week 23 Day 5 Devotions: Reread Psalm 23:4 and the following verses about protection and guidance.

Lamentations 3:58 *O Lord, You have pleaded my soul's cause [You have guided my way and protected me]; You have rescued and redeemed my life.*

Psalm 32:7 *You are my hiding place; You, Lord, protect me from trouble; You surround me with songs and shouts of deliverance. Selah.*

Psalm 31:3 *Yes, You are my rock and my fortress; For Your name's sake You will lead me and guide me.*

Give 1 specific example of a way God has protected you.

_____

_____

_____

_____

Give 1 specific way God has guided you.

_____

_____

_____

_____

Isn't it wonderful how you can look at examples from your own life that prove the Bible is true? Sometimes we forget to remember what He has done because our present situation blocks our view or because we did not receive the answer or outcome we prayed for. However, it is important to look back and praise Him for what He has done so that we do not become bitter or ungrateful and so that we have hope.

Week 23 Day 6 Devotions: Reread Psalm 23:6 and the following verses about dwelling with God.

Psalm 27:4 *One thing I have asked of the Lord, and that I will seek: That I may dwell in the house of the Lord [in His presence] all the days of my life, to gaze upon the beauty [the delightful loveliness and majestic grandeur] of the Lord and to meditate in His temple.*

Psalm 91:9-11 *Because you have made the LORD, [who is] my refuge, Even the Most High, your dwelling place, No evil will befall you, nor will any plague come near your tent. For He will command His angels in regard to you, to protect and defend and guard you in all your ways [of obedience and service].*

Psalm 61:4 *Let me dwell in Your tent forever; Let me take refuge in the shelter of Your wings. Selah.*

Do you choose daily to dwell with God and make Him your dwelling place? _____

Don't be ashamed if life gets busy and takes your focus off Him. Pray that the Holy Spirit will alert you when it happens and then correct it immediately. You don't have to stop and do a 30-minute devotion if you're at work or in the car. You can quote a Bible verse, listen to a Christian song, or just whisper something like: "I love you, God. Be with me." "Thank you, Father. Every good thing I have is from you." It only takes a moment to turn your focus back to Him. What does God promise for those who make God their dwelling place?

_____

_____

_____

_____

Week 23 Day 7 Devotions: reread Psalm 23:6 and the following verses about anointing.

Leviticus 8:12 Then he poured some of the anointing oil on Aaron's head and anointed him, to consecrate him.

1 John 2:27 As for you, the anointing [the special gift, the preparation] which you received from Him remains [permanently] in you, and you have no need for anyone to teach you. But just as His anointing teaches you [giving you insight through the presence of the Holy Spirit] about all things, and is true and is not a lie, and just as His anointing has taught you, you must remain in Him [being rooted in Him, knit to Him].

Luke 4:18 "THE SPIRIT OF THE LORD IS UPON ME (the Messiah), BECAUSE HE HAS ANOINTED ME TO PREACH THE GOOD NEWS TO THE POOR. HE HAS SENT ME TO ANNOUNCE RELEASE (pardon, forgiveness) TO THE CAPTIVES, AND RECOVERY OF SIGHT TO THE BLIND, TO SET FREE THOSE WHO ARE OPPRESSED (downtrodden, bruised, crushed by tragedy),

In Leviticus 8 the anointing represented Aaron being _____, which means he was dedicated or set apart. God anoints you in this way when you receive Jesus as your savior.

Everyone who becomes a Christian also has the anointing described in 1 John 2, which is

_____

_____

What does His anointing teach you and how?

_____

_____

List 3 specific things that the Holy Spirit has taught you.

_____

_____

_____

Week 24 Day 1: Psalm 24

¹The earth is the Lord's, and the fullness of it, the world, and those who dwell in it.
² For He has founded it upon the seas
And established it upon the streams and the rivers.
³ Who may ascend onto the mountain of the Lord? And who may stand in His holy place?
⁴ He who has clean hands and a pure heart, Who has not lifted up his soul to what is false, Nor has sworn [oaths] deceitfully.
⁵ He shall receive a blessing from the Lord, And righteousness from the God of his salvation.
⁶ This is the generation (description) of those who diligently seek Him and require Him as their greatest need, who seek Your face, even [as did] Jacob. Selah.
⁷ Lift up your heads, O gates, And be lifted up, ancient doors, That the King of glory may come in.
⁸ Who is the King of glory? The Lord strong and mighty, The Lord mighty in battle.
⁹ Lift up your heads, O gates, And lift them up, ancient doors, That the King of glory may come in.
¹⁰ Who is [He then] this King of glory? The Lord of hosts, He is the King of glory [who rules over all creation with His heavenly armies]. Selah.

As I researched this Psalm's background, I found some interesting nuggets that I would like to share with you briefly before we get to the focus, which I was led to through prayer while writing this devotion. This Psalm was most likely written when the Ark of the Covenant was being returned to the City of David after having been taken by the Philistines and then placed in the house of Obed-Edum. The Ark represented the presence and provision of God among and for His beloved, chosen people. David loved and longed for God's presence.

In 2 Samuel 6, we see that David gathered the people together to celebrate the Ark's return. He danced, played music and sang, and all of Israel shouted. David offered a burnt offering and gave everyone gathered in the streets bread, meat, and cake. Psalm 24 is thought to have been chanted by the people on that day. Verses 7-10 were the last part of the chorus repeated for emphasis and to alert us to the importance of what was being spoken.

David commanded the gates and the doors to be lifted up so that the King of glory could come in. The Ark returning to the tabernacle was a symbol of God returning to His rightful place in the city. It was also representative of Jesus entering into Heaven after His 40 days on Earth following the resurrection (Jesus was the Lord of glory as we see in 1 Cor. 2:8 and James 2:1). As Jesus completed His purpose on Earth, the church was born. The lifting up of the gates is then also illustrative of mankind opening itself up to make room for Jesus to rule and reign in His rightful place in our hearts.

Our acknowledgement of verses 1-2 that God is the Creator and we belong to Him is the first step to opening our hearts. The second is to acknowledge Jesus' accomplished work on the cross and receive Him through our open gates with shouts of rejoicing. Finally, the next step is to "diligently (conscientiously and thoroughly) seek (pursue) Him and require Him as our greatest need." (vs 6)

Prayer: Heavenly Father, Creator and ruler over all the earth and those who dwell in it, we acknowledge you and accept what Jesus has done on the cross. We open our hearts wide for you to dwell in us. Rule and reign in our lives. Purify our hands, our hearts, and our lips. Make us a mirror of your saving grace and glorious favor so that those around us will see you and be drawn to you. We pray that our nation's leaders, judges, school leaders, and ____(name people you want to see saved) will open their hearts to you and allow you to do a mighty work in them. We thank you for your blessings and the hope of seeing you in Heaven one day. We shout our praises before you unashamedly! You are our king, and we honor you. It is in your name we pray, Amen.

As He enters into the "Holy of Holies," now our very innermost selves, He sets up His kingdom inside of us and dwells there (Eph. 3:17, Romans 8:10). Because He is pure and holy and living in us, we will become more like Him (2 Cor. 3:17-18) with clean hands, a pure heart, and truthful lips (vs. 4). He saves us, makes us righteous, and blesses us (vs. 5). This will enable us to be able to "stand in His holy place" (vs. 3) when we die and go to Heaven.

I would like to focus the rest of this lesson on verse 4 of this Psalm. The amplified Bible refers us to Matthew 5:8 where Jesus is giving His famous Sermon on the Mount, "Blessed (happy, enviably fortunate, and spiritually prosperous-possessing the happiness produced by the experience of God's favor and especially conditioned by the revelation of His grace, regardless of their outward conditions) are the pure in heart, for they shall see God!" Someone who is pure in heart is defined as having integrity, moral courage, and godly character. These people are blessed and happy because they are spiritually prosperous.

They are spiritually prosperous because they have personally experienced God- His presence and grace. They have experienced these things because they opened their heart to Him and have allowed Him to purify them, as we discussed previously.

People with a pure heart can see God for who He really is. Impurities in the heart (sin) are like smudges and scratches on your glasses. Those impurities cannot let us see 20/20 because they distort our vision. Likewise, impurities in the heart affect our perspective, among other things such as our attitude, thoughts, words and actions. We cannot truly see God if our perspective is skewed by sin.

Take for example one of my favorite quotes from The Chronicles of Narnia: *The Magicians Nephew*. In this scene, the children, the cabby, and their uncle are witnessing Aslan, an archetype or representative of God, sing the world of Narnia into existence.

"'Hush!' said the Cabby. They all listened. In the darkness something was happening at last. A voice had begun to sing. It was very far away and Digory found it hard to decide from what direction it was coming. Sometimes it seemed to come from all directions at once. Sometimes he almost thought it was coming out of the earth beneath them. Its lower notes were deep enough to be the voice of the earth herself. There were no words. There was hardly even a tune. But it was, beyond comparison, the most beautiful noise he had ever heard. It was so beautiful he could hardly bear it... 'Gawd!' said the Cabby. 'Ain't it lovely?'

Then two wonders happened at the same moment. One was that the voice was suddenly joined by other voices; more voices than you could possibly count. They were in harmony with it, but far higher up the scale: cold, tingling, silvery voices. The second wonder was that the blackness overhead, all at once, was blazing with stars. They didn't come out gently one by one, as they do on a summer evening. One moment there had been nothing but darkness; next moment a thousand, thousand points of light leaped out – single stars, constellations, and planets, brighter and bigger than any in our world. There were no clouds. The new stars and the new voices began at exactly the same time. If you had seen and heard it, as Digory did, you would have felt quite certain that it was the stars themselves who were singing, and that it was the First Voice, the deep one, which had made them appear and made them sing. 'Glory be!' said the Cabby. 'I'd ha' been a better man all my life if I'd known there were things like this.'

...Far away, and down near the horizon, the sky began to turn grey. A light wind, very fresh, began to stir. The sky, in that one place, grew slowly and steadily paler. You could see shapes of hills standing up dark against it. All the time the Voice went on singing...The eastern sky changed from white to pink and from pink to gold. The Voice rose and rose, till all the air was shaking with it. And just as it swelled to the mightiest and most glorious sound it had yet produced, the sun arose.

Digory had never seen such a sun...You could imagine that it laughed for joy as it came up. And as its beams shot across the land the travelers could see for the first time what sort of place they were in. It was a valley through which a broad, swift river wound its way, flowing eastward towards the sun. Southward there were mountains, northward there were lower hills. But it was a valley of mere earth, rock and water; there was not a tree, not a bush, not a blade of grass to be seen. The earth was of many colours: they were fresh, hot and vivid. They made you feel excited; until you saw the Singer himself, and then you forgot everything else. It was a Lion. Huge, shaggy, and bright it stood facing the risen sun. Its mouth was wide open in song and it was about three hundred yards away."

The children were amazed and awestruck. It was magical, beautiful, and glorious to them, but to the uncle it was horrifying. "It had not made at all the same impression on him as on the cabby and the children. For what you see and hear depends a good deal on where you are standing: it also depends on what sort of person you are."

The scene depicts perfectly what impurities in the heart can do and the affect they can have on the person. Because the children and cabby were pure, they could see the truth of who Aslan was and what he was doing, but the uncle could not. Because the uncle was seeing through an impure heart, his vision was distorted and therefore his perspective on the happenings was as well. Because his perspective was distorted, his emotions and reactions were also askew.

There was nothing Aslan could do for him, "'He thinks great folly, child,' said Aslan. 'This world is bursting with life for these few days because the song with which I called it into life still hangs in the air and rumbles in the ground. It will not be so for long. But I cannot tell that to this old sinner, and I cannot comfort him either; he has made himself unable to hear my voice. If I spoke to him, he would hear only growlings and roarings. Oh, Adam's son, how cleverly you defend yourself against all that might do you good!'" The uncle would require a heart change, which would be completely up to him to recognize and request.

One problem with distortion is that it becomes deception if not put in check by the Holy Spirit. It is up to us to request help with this and to see things through God's eyes with the help of the Holy Spirit at work in us. Deception changes people's thinking and action. Deception is rampant in our world today. It is grabbing hold of our young people and even Christians and they are becoming just like the uncle from *The Magician's Nephew.*

Only salvation can set someone free from deception. It cannot be reasoned out of the person, believer or unbeliever (yes, believers can become deceived by Satan and the things of the world if they do not consistently, consciously pursue God and make Him a necessity in their life vs.6). We can and should present the truth, but it is the Holy Spirit who opens the eyes and illuminates the truth so that the mind can be free, and the heart can change. Oh, and what a change it can produce! A glorious revelation of God's favor and grace (Matt 5:8) will purify our hands, hearts, and lips, bless us, and allow us to see God here on Earth and in Heaven (vs.3-5). This is what seeing God truly means, and those who do are blessed.

Who is the Lord? He is the King of glory, strong and mighty! Who is the King of glory? He is the Lord of hosts, creator, and ruler over all! Won't you lift up the door of your heart for Him today!

Week 24 Day 1 Notes for Psalm 24: Which verse stood out to you the most and why?

_____

_____

_____

_____

What important life lesson can you apply from this Psalm?

_____

_____

_____

_____

Week 24 Day 2 Devotions: Reread Psalm 24:1 and the following verse on everything belonging to God.

1 Corinthians 10:26 *For the [whole] earth is the Lord's, and everything that is in it.*

Psalm 89:11 *The heavens are Yours, the earth also is Yours; The world and all that is in it, You have founded and established them.*

Deuteronomy 10:14 *Behold, the heavens and the highest of heavens belong to the LORD your God, the earth and all that is in it.*

List 5 people who are most important to you.

_____

_____

List 5 things you have, other than people, that are most valuable to you.

_____

_____

_____

Lift these things up to your powerful Father in prayer. Commit them to Him, for they are His already. Thank Him for them, and pray for His protection and continued blessings.

Week 24 Day 3 Devotions: Reread Psalm 24:2 and the following verses on God as creator.

Isaiah 42:5 *This is what God the LORD says, He who created the heavens and stretched them out, Who spread out the earth and its produce, Who gives breath to the people on it And spirit to those who walk on it, "I am the LORD, I have called You (the Messiah) in righteousness [for a righteous purpose], I will also take You by the hand and keep watch over You, And I will appoint You as a covenant to the people [Israel], As a light to the nations (Gentiles),*

Proverbs 30:4 *Who has ascended into heaven and descended? Who has gathered the wind in His fists? Who has bound the waters in His garment? Who has established all the ends of the earth? What is His name, and what is His Son's name? Certainly you know!*

2 Peter 3:5 *For they willingly forget [the fact] that the heavens existed long ago by the word of God, and the earth was formed but of water and by water,*

According to Peter, some people willingly forget that God is the mighty creator. They choose to forget or choose not to believe. I want to encourage you to "stop and smell the roses." Take time to notice, admire, and praise God for His creation. That same creator of Heaven and Earth has also created a plan of salvation for all people. What does Isaiah 42 say about this?

_____

_____

_____

Make a conscious choice to remember and share what you have learned about God and His salvation plan.

Week 24 Day 4 Devotions: Reread Psalm 24:4-5 and the following verses on blessings from God for staying clean/pure.

Matthew 5:8 *"Blessed [anticipating God's presence, spiritually mature] are the pure in heart [those with integrity, moral courage, and godly character], for they will see God.*

2 Samuel 22:21 *"The LORD has dealt with me according to my righteousness; According to the cleanness of my hands He has rewarded me.*

Psalm 119:1 *How blessed and favored by God are those whose way is blameless [those with personal integrity, the upright, the guileless], Who walk in the law [and who are guided by the precepts and revealed will] of the LORD.*

How is "blessed" defined in Matthew 5? _____

How are "pure in heart" and "blameless" defined in Matthew 5 and Psalm 119?

_____

_____

_____

No one is perfect. You are made perfect through Jesus' blood shed on the cross. Although, our actions do speak volumes, God ultimately judges your heart. Intentions do matter. How do you at least aim yourself in the right direction according to Psalm 119?

_____

_____

Week 24 Day 5 Devotions: Reread Psalm 24:6 and the following verses about seeking God.

1 Chronicles 16:11 *Seek the LORD and His strength; Seek His face continually [longing to be in His presence].*

Jeremiah 29:13 *Then [with a deep longing] you will seek Me and require Me [as a vital necessity] and [you will] find Me when you search for Me with all your heart.*

Psalm 63:1 *O God, You are my God; with deepest longing I will seek You; My soul [my life, my very self] thirsts for You, my flesh longs and sighs for You, In a dry and weary land where there is no water.*

Be careful not to seek God just for what He can give you. 1 Chronicles 16 tells you to seek His

_____ and _____ –long to be in His presence.

Jeremiah says that God promises that when you seek Him _____

_____ you will find Him. He will not hide His face and grace from you.

Oh, that we would thirst after God with deep longing and with everything inside us as David did. Pray right now for God to deepen your desire for Him.

Week 24 Day 6 Devotions: Reread Psalm 24:10 and the following verses about the King of glory.

Luke 19:38 *shouting, "Blessed (celebrated, praised) is the King who comes in the name of the Lord! Peace in heaven and glory (majesty, splendor) in the highest [heaven]!"*

1 Thessalonians 2:12 *to live lives [of honor, moral courage, and personal integrity] worthy of the God who [saves you and] calls you into His own kingdom and glory.*

1 Timothy 1:17 *Now to the King of the ages [eternal], immortal, invisible, the only God, be honor and glory forever and ever. Amen.*

Jesus is coming again! Celebrate and praise Him! In 1 Thessalonians 3, He beckons you to live a life of

_____ so that you can live with Him in His eternal kingdom and glory.

According to Psalm 24:8, 10 and 1 Timothy 1, who is the King of Glory (describe Him)?

_____

_____

_____

Week 24 Day 7 Devotions: Reread Psalm 24:10 and the following verses about the Lord of hosts.

Amos 4:13 *For behold, He who forms the mountains and creates the wind and declares to man what are His thoughts, He who makes the dawn into darkness and treads on the heights of the earth— The Lord God of hosts is His name.*

Zechariah 2:8-11 *For thus says the LORD of hosts, "After glory He has sent Me against the nations which plunder you—for he who touches you, touches the apple of His eye. Behold, I will wave my hand over them and they shall become plunder for their own slaves. Then you shall know (recognize, understand fully) that the LORD of hosts has sent Me. Sing for joy and rejoice, O Daughter of Zion; for behold, I am coming, and I will dwell in your midst," declares the LORD. Many nations shall join themselves to the LORD in that day and shall be My people. And I will dwell in your midst, and you shall know (recognize, understand fully) that the LORD of hosts has sent Me to you.*

Matthew 25:31 *"But when the Son of Man comes in His glory and majesty and all the angels with Him, then He will sit on the throne of His glory.*

As we bring our study of the first 24 chapters of Psalms to a close, let us leave with the most important idea that David shares with us, the most important and central idea of the entire Bible—God loves you and sent His only son to die the most wretched death so that you could be saved. The God described by David all throughout the Psalms and in the past 24 weeks of daily devotions desires you to open the gates of your heart and give Him full reign to love you, guide you, and protect you. One day He will come again, as described in Zechariah 2 and Matthew 25, as the Lord of Hosts—the Lord of heavenly armies—and we will reign victoriously with Him forever. Reflect on these thoughts and verses for a few moments and write down your reaction to them.

_____

_____

_____

_____

_____